Haynes
Moulby
Post
R.D.

Topic

uneducated man
1. satisfactit
2. education - go on with it.

$\cdot 2\overline{5\smash{)}110,000}$ .99%
1000

19 — Blair & Gerber — The thru Aim for Written
227 See what things he uses — analyze the same.
infinitives

Chp. 7 Effective sentences - Minimum
130 - 155

Non — Test

Structural Grammar

FOR BUILDING SENTENCES

W. Otto Birk
UNIVERSITY OF COLORADO

D. C. HEATH AND COMPANY : Boston

TO   *David William Schodt*
AND *Mary Margaret McComb*

PREFACE

This book aims to explain the essentials of grammar as a means of writing sentences. Because of this purpose, it is concerned neither with the historical aspects of the subject nor with moot problems of usage. On the other hand, it is not another of the numerous workbooks, which tend to break up the subject and thus give a student the impression that it consists of isolated rules and exercises. Inasmuch as many students leave high school with this confusion of fragments, the purpose of this book is to provide a review that will integrate the subject and focus it upon its useful function of making sentences.

The book, therefore, deals primarily with the structural aspects of grammar. Matters of "interior finish" it does not ignore, but it considers them of secondary importance. Recently they have been discussed thoroughly by researchers in the use of language — so thoroughly that many people seem to have the impression that the only purpose in studying grammar is to find out whether they should say, for example, "It is I" or "It is me"; and since they are told that all of the books have been pigheadedly wrong about these matters, they naturally conclude that grammar is useless.

Nevertheless, sentences are still made by means of grammar; and the inexperienced writer should therefore understand its structural principles. Just as the builder of houses should know the materials at his disposal and how and when he should use them, either singly or in combination, so the builder of sentences should understand his materials, words and the parts of speech; and he should know how to put them together into subject and predicate and how to use them singly and in such groups as phrases and clauses. These structural problems, always in their relationship to building sentences, are the dominant concern of this book.

v

In order to achieve its purpose, the text has been divided into three parts, designated as A, B, and C. Section A is basic. It discusses all of the elements of a sentence; but even though it takes up one element at a time and treats it in a separate Study Unit, its total aim is to give a unified, coherent discussion of sentence structure so that the student should complete it with a comprehensive view of how a sentence is made. For this reason, the first section is kept as free as possible from any unnecessarily lengthy discussion of matters that might interfere with the continuity of the picture. Two of these matters are phrases and clauses. They are defined in Section A, and are referred to whenever they must be; but a full discussion is left for Section B, which treats these two groups exclusively and thoroughly.

In addition to freeing Section A from interruption, this segregation has two advantages. First, it emphasizes these important aspects of sentence structure, which always cause students much trouble; and it makes the discussion of them readily available, so that a student who needs special instruction can get it without having to pick it out of different parts of the text — or having the instructor find it for him. Second, inasmuch as a misunderstanding of phrases and clauses results in two serious faults in sentence structure, the period and the comma faults, this segregation facilitates instruction in how to overcome them. To this end, the discussion in Section B is directed toward the difficult problem of helping the student recognize sentences.

Section C deals with matters of a different kind within the sentence, problems involving agreement and case. These also are mentioned elsewhere; but since a student often needs concentrated instruction in them, the segregation helps him to get it readily.

A word should be said for the general treatment. The purpose of the book is not to state succinct rules, but to explain principles. At any point in the text, this explanation is given as fully as necessary, even though it may repeat something mentioned elsewhere. The reason is to provide understanding as it is needed without interrupting the discussion with cross reference. Occasionally attention is called to a fuller treatment in other parts, but only for further study. These explanations, moreover, are made concrete by numerous illustrations, so that the functional emphasis of the book is constantly maintained.

Though it is not a workbook, the text has numerous exercises, some at the end of each Study Unit and extra, comprehensive exercises at the end of the book. These are of two kinds: the conventional sentence exercises and another that might be called theme exercises. The former are rather easy to do, as are most exercises of this type; and so they ought to be used first. The second are more difficult. Inasmuch as they consist of connected discourse, the problems of grammar that they illustrate are less obvious, and thus they require the student to be more alert. As compensation, however, they are far more interesting to both student and instructor. The two types may be used as quizzes, though they are not designed as such. They are intended for use in the classroom, as a means of providing a review and giving the student a better understanding of what he learned in each Study Unit.

Many students and colleagues, through classroom work and casual discussions, have contributed to the point of view and the treatment of this book. I should mention every one of them if I remembered them individually and had space for their names. Since I do not, I here acknowledge my debt. Others have helped so directly and constantly that I am fortunately able to thank each one. Dr. E. A. Cross, of the Colorado State College of Education, who has for many years inspired me by his example as teacher and author, read early portions of the manuscript and encouraged me to complete it. Among my colleagues at the University of Colorado, the following members of the English staff in the College of Engineering helped in many ways, but particularly by using some of the exercises in their classes and suggesting revisions: C. K. Arnold, John Barker, Mrs. L. W. Cook, William W. Graham, H. W. Hawk, H. Harold Kelley, R. E. Kilbride, Waino S. Nyland, Robert F. Scott, and Paul V. Thompson. Professor Kelley, in addition, read the manuscript, advised me about revisions, and read proof. Professor Thompson followed the manuscript through from its early stages, consulted with me frequently, and read the proof. I should say, of course, that inasmuch as I prepared the manuscript and read the proof last, I am responsible for all of the faults in the book. The merits of it the foregoing share with me, as do also the college editors of D. C. Heath and Company, who went beyond the requirements of their positions to be cooperative and helpful.

CONTENTS

ix

Micrimmon

504
Uses of comma, semi-colon, colon,

all punctuation — theory of it

INTRODUCTORY UNIT FOR STUDENTS
A Foreword on Grammar

A Foreword on Grammar

Did you ever try — in your grade school years, perhaps — to make a language that you could use in exchanging secrets with a classmate? If you did, you recall how handicapped you were in saying what you wanted to say. You were never sure that your correspondent understood your special words as you did. Before you could exchange a single thought, you had to decide upon certain symbols or combinations of symbols that you called words; and then you had to agree upon the meanings of these words. The chances are that you soon gave up your private language and accepted the hazards of communicating your secrets in one that everybody could understand. But if you and your friend had been forced by circumstances to use this private language and no other, you would have been in no worse predicament than if the two of you had been marooned as babies on different parts of an uninhabited island. Had you met, after ten or fifteen years of association with the animals of the woods, your grunts and growls would scarcely have led to conversation. Before you could have exchanged the simplest thoughts, outside those expressed by pantomime, you would have had to agree upon a language. In talking to yourself, of course, you could have called a lion an "oompah" or even a "monkey"; but if your newly found acquaintance always had said "oompah" in referring to a bird and "monkey" in referring to an elephant, the two of you would have had a bit of difficulty in gossiping about your neighbors. If, then, you had wanted to share your thoughts with each other, you would have been forced to do what you despaired of doing in grade school: you would have been forced to make a language.

In this task, the chances are that you would have followed the same general course that has been taken in the development of our existing languages. At first you would have made use of gestures and pantomime and perhaps even drawn pictures of objects; and then, as your thoughts became more complicated and more abstract, you would have devised spoken symbols. You would have produced words by combining sounds in various ways, and you would have agreed upon what the words meant and how they were to be used together. This agreement, you would have discovered, was positively necessary if each was to understand the statements of the other. Eventually, however, the words would have become so numerous and the usages so varied that you could not have trusted your memory to retain all of them; and so you would have devised written symbols to represent the spoken ones. Still later you would have made dictionaries and grammars.

To be sure, you would not have lived long enough to do all this; but if you had, you would merely have been reliving the struggle that man has had — though he has been largely unaware of it — to develop a device for thinking and for expressing his thoughts. This device, of course, is called language.

What, then, is language? If we define it as a device for expressing thought, we find that there are many languages. Algebra, for instance, is in this sense a language, as is also mechanical drawing. By means of symbols, agreed upon by all who use them, both of these devices express thoughts — and they also supply the patterns by which thinking is done. The language, however, that is understood by most people, instead of by only a specially trained group, is the one that employs words. It is a language in which our grunts and growls and chuckles — our words — have come to have a socialized meaning; that is, they have a meaning that is understood and accepted by most people. Essentially, it is nothing more than words; in use, however, it is words that are put together in an orderly manner. They are not merely strung side by side like beads on a wire, but are arranged like the pieces of a puzzle map, so that when each one is in its proper place, the group of them forms a unit that expresses a design — or, as we should say, that expresses a thought.

If you want to express your thought, then, you must learn how words ought to be put together. Fortunately, you do not need to go through the laborious process of beginning a new language by agreeing with your neighbors upon definitions and rules. For a long time this task has been going on, so that you now have within your use a systematized language with rules already prepared. Of course, these rules are not unalterable, and they are not so universally true and definite as "two times two equals four" — nor can they ever be. As long as a language changes, as every living language is bound to do, some of the rules for its use must change. Yet these changes take place so slowly that the fundamental rules have been the same for many generations and are certain to remain essentially the same as long as you live. Since the change has been so slow as to be scarcely noticeable, millions of people have known these rules and have followed them in expressing their thoughts; millions more know them now, and are using them; so, if you want to share the thoughts of past and present generations, and if you want to share your thoughts with your contemporaries, you must learn the rules.

The chief purpose of this book is to help you master the fundamental rules and principles that you will need in order to group words into a pattern that forms the essential unit of thought. This unit, of course, is the sentence. For complete expression, other units are obviously necessary, such as the paragraph and the whole article; but these units are nothing more than collections of properly arranged sentences. Without the sentence they could no more exist than water could without hydrogen and oxygen. If, then, you master the fundamentals of the sentence, you are equipped to undertake the advanced tasks of composition; if you do not master them, you will never write with confidence and ease — or even correctness.

What is a sentence? To answer this question fully is the purpose of the whole discussion that follows, but that discussion is based on the fundamental idea that the aim of a sentence is to state a thought. This aim is attained by bringing suitable words into proper relationship with one another. Whenever these words do not state a complete thought — that is, all of one thought — they do not make a sentence; and whenever they state more than one thought, they make more than a sentence. A sentence must state a thought — one complete thought, but no more than one thought. Do not lose this point of view.

The principles followed in using words so that they express a complete thought are the subject of grammar; and since the following discussion seeks to explain these principles, it explains grammar. Its purpose, however, is not to tell you all that you might know about the subject. To use grammar, you do not need to know all about it; furthermore, you already know much about it, because you have studied grammar more or less formally for many years. For these reasons the purpose of this book is to emphasize the essentials of grammar needed in writing a sentence and to focus them so that you can see clearly how they are used. Remember, therefore, when you encounter explanations of grammar in the following pages, that they are intended not to instruct you merely in the technicalities of this subject, but to enable you to express a thought — that is, to write a sentence.

Section A
How a Sentence Is Constructed

The Materials of a Sentence: Parts of Speech

1. You have expressed a thought by means of a sentence only when you have used suitable words in their proper relationship to one another. These "suitable" words are the materials of which sentences are made. They are grouped into eight classes, called parts of speech: *noun*, *pronoun*, *verb*, *adjective*, *adverb*, *conjunction*, *preposition*, and *interjection*. Since we shall have to refer to these terms frequently in our discussion, you should now learn a brief definition of each.

Noun

2. A *noun* is a word used to name a person, place, or thing.

3. All nouns are classified as either *common* or *proper*. A *common noun* is a word used to name all members of a class of persons, places, or things. A *proper noun* is a word used as the specific name of an individual member of a class of persons, places, or things. A proper noun begins with a capital letter. Both types are illustrated in the following sentences:

> *Caroline* was *chairman* of a *committee* to provide *recreation* for young *children*.
> *Nederland* is a small *town* in the *mountains* of *Colorado*.
> *Keats* said that *truth* and *beauty* are the same.
> *Christianity* is a *religion* that originated along the eastern *shores* of the *Mediterranean*.

9

4. A group of words may function as a single noun, either common or proper, as in the following sentences:

> *Dove, Smith and Company* sell all kinds of dogs.
>
> *Colorado Springs* is near the foot of *Pikes Peak*, on the eastern side of the *Rocky Mountains*, overlooking the *Great Plains*.
>
> The former *errand boy* in the office of *Zenith Airlines, Inc.*, is now a member of the *House of Representatives*.

Pronoun

5. A *pronoun* is a word generally used as a substitute for a noun in order to refer to a person or thing without naming it.

> Robert is very punctual; *he* arrived at 10 precisely.
>
> This tennis racket is old but *it* is in good condition.
>
> Mary is the girl *who* was elected president of the class.

6. The word for which the pronoun stands is called its *antecedent*. In the preceding sentences *Robert*, *racket*, and *girl* are the antecedents of the italicized pronouns. The antecedent may be a pronoun instead of a noun.

> *You who* are here will be served first. (*You* is the antecedent of *who*.)
>
> *Everyone* should bring *his* tray to the serving table. (*Everyone* is the antecedent of *his*.)

The antecedent may be compound, consisting of two or more words.

> Open the *doors* and *windows* as soon as *they* are unlocked.
>
> *He* and *she* went together to see *their* friend.

7. A pronoun may have no expressed antecedent. It may refer to a person or thing that is readily understood without being named, or it may refer to an expression which follows or to the expected answer to a question.

I do not understand *you.*
Few can do the work expertly.
That is the building where John works.
Who came here tonight?

8. The various kinds of pronouns will be discussed in Study Unit 2.

9. NOTE: Since nouns and pronouns have the same function of designating persons or objects, one term is often used in referring to either. This term is *substantive.* It is used even more broadly, as you will see later, to refer to any word or group of words that functions in a sentence as a noun.

Verb

10. A *verb* is a word or group of words that asserts the action or condition of someone or something.

The wheel *rotates* rapidly.
The door *is* open.
They *have gone* home.
They *will be* hungry when they arrive.
We *have* now *been coming* here for vacations for five years.

11. Observe that when a verb is a group of words (usually called a *verb phrase*) its members may be separated by other parts of speech, as in the last sentence above. In each verb phrase there is one word that expresses the essential action or condition (*gone* in the third sentence, *be* in the fourth, and *coming* in the fifth); the other words are called *auxiliary verbs*, that is, "aiding" or "helping" verbs. You will learn more about them in Study Unit 5.

Adjective

12. An *adjective* is a word that describes or defines a noun in order to amplify or restrict its meaning. Since, in performing this function, it changes somewhat the meaning of the noun, an adjective is said to *modify* a noun.

13. Adjectives are classified as either *descriptive* or *definitive*. *Descriptive adjectives* give the qualities of nouns: *bright, dismal, green, lively, rough, succulent, harsh,* etc. *Definitive adjectives* indicate how many or which members of a group or class a noun refers to: *a, an, the* (these three are called *articles*), *this, that, many, few, five, tenth,* etc.

> *The new* books had *red, green,* and *yellow* bindings.
> *Many expert* craftsmen work on *these tedious* jobs.
> *A tall, slender* shaft was erected by *the grateful* citizens.

Adverb

14. An *adverb* is a word used to modify a verb, an adjective, or another adverb. Generally it answers the question "How?" "When?" "Where?" "To what degree?" or "To what extent?"

> Elizabeth skates *gracefully*. (Modifies the verb *skates*.)
> The guests arrived *early*. (Modifies the verb *arrived*.)
> The color is *too* blue. (Modifies the adjective *blue*.)
> The art dealer sent us these *unusually* long crayons. (Modifies the adjective *long*.)
> We must hang this picture *very carefully*. (The adverb *very* modifies the adverb *carefully*, which in turn modifies the verb *must hang*.)
> The airplane flew *unbelievably fast*. (The adverb *unbelievably* modifies the adverb *fast*, which in turn modifies the verb *flew*.)

Preposition

15. A *preposition* is a word used to connect a substantive, which is called the object of the preposition, with some other word in the sentence and to show the relationship between them.

16. In the following sentences observe how the italicized prepositions express different relationships between *house* (the object of the prepositions) and *played*.

The children played *behind* the house.
The children played *in front of* the house.
The children played *in* the house.
The children played *outside* the house.

17. A preposition may have a compound object.

We built a wall between the *house* and the *garage*.

Conjunction

18. A *conjunction* similarly connects words or groups of words and shows the relationship between them, but its connective functions are more varied than are those of prepositions.

19. Conjunctions that connect words or groups of words of equal importance in the sentence are called <u>coordinate conjunctions</u>.

Ferns *and* roses decorated the stage.
We came home tired *but* happy.
I can see you before class *or* after lunch.
One road went to Tipton *and* the other went to Freeport.

20. Conjunctions that join a less important part of a sentence to a more important part are called <u>subordinate conjunctions</u>.

John rode in the airplane *because* Fred urged him.
Though the motor had stopped, the pilot landed without mishap.
The airplane stopped *when* the gas line broke.

Interjection

21. An *interjection* is a word used as an exclamation to express some emotion such as surprise, fear, joy, sorrow, or anger.

Oh! I hit my finger.
Alas, he is gone.
Whew! This day is scorching hot.
Bravo! You have won.

Classification Determined by Use

22. Undoubtedly you have observed in these definitions that a word is classified as one or another part of speech not necessarily because of its form but because of its *use in the sentence*. Two or more parts of speech may have the same form, as in the following sentences:

> The *man* was tall. (Noun)   We alone must *man* the ship. (Verb)
> Birds *fly*. (Verb)   A *fly* lit on his nose. (Noun)
> The *fast* train has left. (Adjective)   You must drive *fast*. (Adverb)   The *fast* will last three days. (Noun)   They *fast* every Friday. (Verb)

Moreover, a word that is normally classed as one part of speech may be used as another. Any part of speech can be used as a noun in such a sentence as "*Run* is a verb." Most adjectives can be used as nouns in sentences of the pattern "The *good* die young," "The *industrious* rarely end in poverty"; similarly, most nouns can be used as adjectives in such sentences as "The *Saturday* concerts are over," "The *taxation* problem is severe." Many other examples of such functional shift might be given.

23. When you are trying, therefore, to determine what part of speech a word is, you must study its use in the sentence in which it occurs.

EXERCISE 1.   Identification of Parts of Speech

In the following sentences tell what part of speech each word is:

1. Bees fly in a straight line.
2. I have been reading two interesting books about the Puritans in America.
3. Whew! When the plane flew out over the lake where the

wind was strong, I heard a sound like a crack, and I feared that the aviator would be killed.

4. We have read all of the good books and magazines that the little village library provides, but those, alas, are not many.

5. We skated regularly on the big pond at the mill until the ice thawed.

6. As we stood idly in the valley and looked at the top of the high hill, we saw distinctly the outline of a huge cave.

7. Tall trees flourished in the valley and on the low hills, but only a few gnarled trees and dwarfed shrubs grew here and there on the top of this high hill.

8. We looked diligently and hopefully for a path to the top of the hill, but we found none.

9. We climbed the hill slowly because the underbrush was thick and a tangle of vines hung loosely between the trees.

10. The cave, we have since that time discovered, is exceedingly large, like the great room in a castle, with six enormous stone pillars along the open side.

The Materials of a Sentence:
Kinds of Pronouns

The matter of Form
We recognize them we see the form.
Grammar — structure of language, not function
Rhetoric effective use of grammar.

1. There are five kinds of pronouns: *personal*, *relative*, *interrogative*, *demonstrative*, and *indefinite*.

Personal Pronouns

2. A *personal pronoun* represents a person or thing more specifically than does any other pronoun, because it has a distinct form to indicate each of the three persons — the speaker, the person spoken to, and the person or thing spoken about. In addition, the first and third persons have separate forms to indicate singular and plural number, and the third person singular has a distinct form for each of the three genders.

	SINGULAR	PLURAL
First person	I	we
Second person	you	you
Third person masculine	he	they
feminine	she	they
neuter	it	they

3. Each of the foregoing pronouns, moreover, has still other forms — some more than others — to indicate its function in a sentence. The first person singular, for example, takes the form *I* when the pronoun is the subject or the predicate noun; *my* when it indicates the possessor; and *me* when it is the object of a verb or a preposition. The other pronouns, likewise, take different forms. These

16

forms show what is called *case*, the purpose of which is to indicate the relationship of a substantive to a verb, a preposition, or another substantive.   English substantives have three cases, *nominative*, *possessive*, and *objective*. Their use is illustrated in the sentence, "*I* took *him* with *me* in *my* car."   *I* is related to the verb *took* as a subject and is said to be in the nominative case.   *My* is related to the substantive *car* as possessor, and is therefore in the possessive case.   *Him*, related to *took* as object, and *me*, related to the preposition *with* as object, are in the objective case.   (For fuller discussion of case dealing especially with perplexing problems in usage, turn to Study Unit 20.)

4. All forms of the personal pronoun are given in the following table, which is called a *declension*.   Learn them so that you can identify them unmistakably and use them.

| | SINGULAR | | | PLURAL | | |
	Nom.	Poss.	Obj.	Nom.	Poss.	Obj.
First Person	I	my (mine)	me	we	our (ours)	us
Second Person	you	your (yours)	you	you	your (yours)	you
Third Person						
Masculine	he	his	him	they	their (theirs)	them
Feminine	she	her (hers)	her	they	their (theirs)	them
Neuter	it	its	it	they	their (theirs)	them

COMPOUND PERSONAL PRONOUNS

5. Personal pronouns are combined with the suffix *self* to form *intensive* and *reflexive pronouns*.   Only the following forms, however, appear with this ending.

SINGULAR	PLURAL
myself	ourselves
yourself	yourselves
himself	
herself	themselves
itself	

6. These forms are used as *intensive pronouns* when they emphasize the substantives to which they refer, as in the following sentences:

> We ourselves must take the full responsibility.
> Frank made the boat himself.
> They themselves must give us the information.
> I found the answer myself.

7. The same forms are used as *reflexive pronouns* when they are the objects of verbs or prepositions but refer to (or stand for) the subjects.

> The children entertained themselves.
> Janet hurt herself when her skate came off.
> We divided the candy among ourselves.

8. In addition to personal pronouns, the indefinite pronoun *one* may become a reflexive pronoun.

> One must protect oneself.
> One should ask oneself the question first.

Relative Pronouns

9. *Relative pronouns* are *who, which, that, what,* and *as. Who, which,* and *what* are made into compound relatives by the addition of *ever* or *soever: whoever, whosoever, whichever, whichsoever, whatever, whatsoever.*

10. *Who* and its compounds change their form to indicate case:

> *Nominative:* who, whoever, whosoever
> *Possessive:* whose, whosever, whosesoever
> *Objective:* whom, whomever, whomsoever

11. A relative pronoun is peculiar in that it serves not only as a pronoun but as a connective. As a pronoun it takes the place of a substantive that is its antecedent in

the sentence, and as a connective it joins to that substantive the group of words that it introduces.

> The new chemistry laboratory, which was opened last week, is still not fully equipped. (*Which* takes the place of *laboratory* and also connects with it the subordinate thought that it introduces, "which was opened last week.")

12. *What* and the compound relatives logically include their own antecedents, so that they have no expressed antecedents.

> I do not remember what (= that which) I said.
> Whoever (= anyone who) wishes to speak may do so.

13. *As* is a relative when *such* or *same* is in the clause containing the antecedent:

> He could easily remember such questions as he was asked.
> He answered again the same questions as he was asked before.

Interrogative Pronouns

14. *Interrogative pronouns* are the same in form as three of the relatives: *who* (*whose*, *whom*), *which*, *what*. They differ from the relatives, however, in function. They are used to ask questions, direct and indirect.

> Who is he?
> Whom did you meet?
> Which of those people arrived first?
> What shall we get her for her birthday?
> I should like to know who he is.
> I wonder whom we should ask.

15. Interrogative pronouns do not have expressed antecedents.

16. *Which* and *what* may be used as either pronouns or adjectives; hence you must take care to distinguish be-

tween the two functions. The difference in usage is illustrated in the following sentences:

> Which did he assign? (Pronoun)
> Which lesson did he assign? (Adjective)
> What shall we get her? (Pronoun)
> What gift shall we get her? (Adjective)

Demonstrative Pronouns

17. The *demonstrative pronouns* are *this* (plural *these*), *that* (plural *those*), and *such*. They do not have different forms to indicate case.

18. These pronouns, as their name indicates, "show" or "point to" something — to a word or a thought in the preceding sentence, or directly to a person or thing being discussed.

> This is the building where I work.
> That will be difficult.
> Such are the advantages of the plan.

19. You must take care to distinguish the pronominal use of demonstratives from their use as adjectives.

> This is exciting. (Pronoun)
> This book is exciting. (Adjective)
> That is a novel. (Pronoun)
> That book is a novel. (Adjective)
> Such were their arguments. (Pronoun)
> Such arguments are typical. (Adjective)

Indefinite Pronouns

20. *Indefinite pronouns*, as their name indicates, need not refer to a definite antecedent. Important examples are: *each, both, either, neither, some, all, none, several, any, few, many, other, another, one, someone, somebody, something, everyone, everybody, everything, anyone, anybody, anything.*

21. Most pronouns of this type are either always singular or always plural in meaning, but *one* and *other* form plurals in *s*, and *none* appears in present usage in both singular and plural senses. A few indefinite pronouns have possessive forms in *'s* (singular) or *s'* (plural).

> One came yesterday; the other is (*or* the others are) expected today.
> The ones I like best are these.
> None of the butter is fresh.
> None of the books are interesting.
> Your guess is as good as anyone's.
> Their offices are smaller than the others'.

22. Most of these indefinites can be used as either pronouns or adjectives. Their use is illustrated in the following sentences:

> Neither would yield.   (Pronoun)
> Neither experiment was successful.   (Adjective)
> A few volunteered.   (Pronoun)
> We solved only a few problems.   (Adjective)
> Many are expected.   (Pronoun)
> Many students attended the concert.   (Adjective)

EXERCISE 2.   Identification of Pronouns

Identify the pronouns in the following sentences:

1. We met them at your house last summer when they were visiting you.
2. They remembered all whom they had met at your party.
3. Both of us saw the books that were on my table yesterday, but now neither is there.
4. Who is able now to solve this himself after I have explained it?
5. That is not what I told either of you.

6. When they stopped their car in front of our house, I recognized them instantly.
7. He hurt himself while he repaired his car, which was an obsolete model.
8. We told him what we knew about their plans for a picnic.
9. Who saw either of them put these on my desk?
10. Each came from the same town, but neither knew the other until I introduced them.

EXERCISE 3. Identification of Parts of Speech

Tell what part of speech each word in the following paragraph is:

In a small park that formed a semicircle at the mouth of a cañon in our western mountains, Frank and I saw an unusual performance. Here a man walked a tightrope. This seems ordinary, but it was not. The walls of this cañon, which consisted of solid rock, were high and straight. Between them, from the top of one to the top of the other, stretched a cable, which everybody called a "rope." To us who saw it from the ground it looked like a string. At each end of it was a small platform. On one of these appeared a man in tights. All of us watched him closely. Presently he stepped upon the wire. Before him he carried a long pole, which he moved slightly from side to side. With this, we learned later, he balanced himself. He cautiously took another step, and then another. Like a mechanical toy he stepped forward until he was nearly an equal distance from each side. In the middle of space, we felt, he stopped. He knelt upon one knee, rose, and knelt upon the other. Promptly he rose again, stood still momentarily, and then resumed his walk to the other side. From the little platform he waved, and we filled the cañon with our shouts of approval.

The ~~Design~~ of a Sentence

[handwritten: Pattern or]

[handwritten: 3 Types]

[handwritten: subject / verb]

[handwritten: Subj. | V. | D.O]

[handwritten: S. | V. \ C.]

1. The parts of speech described in Study Units 1 and 2 are the materials you must use in making a sentence. They have work to do in a sentence, each according to its use, and are therefore said to be functional. They work together. Hence you must use them according to a design, or pattern, in which each word is clearly related to the other words. The purpose of this Study Unit is to explain the design of a sentence by showing you how the words in it are related.

2. Though this design varies in different sentences, it always consists basically of relatively few elements. According to the functions they perform, all the words in any sentence fall into one or more of five groups:

   a. Basic elements
   b. Modifying elements
   c. Connective elements
   d. Appositive elements
   e. Independent elements

Many sentences do not contain appositive elements or independent elements, and some do not contain modifying elements or connective elements, but all contain basic elements.

Basic Elements

3. As the name implies, the most important elements are the basic. There are three of these: *subject, verb,* and *complement.*

THE TWO INDISPENSABLE BASIC ELEMENTS
IN EVERY SENTENCE

4. Every sentence must contain the first two of these elements, a subject and a verb.

5. The *subject* is the word or group of words in a sentence that names the person or thing about which the sentence makes a statement. Since it names, it is a substantive.

> The *guard* on our team tossed the ball.
> *Fred* made the score.
> *We* have attended every concert.
> The *Omar Baking Company* made this bread.

6. The *verb*, as basic element, is the word — or group of words — in the sentence that makes the chief statement about the subject. Since the function of this part of speech is to state action or condition, it gives the action or condition of the subject or the action upon the subject.

> Mary *arrived* yesterday.
> John *is sleeping* soundly.
> He *looked* tired.
> The score *was made* in the first quarter.

7. It is easy to see why these two elements are indispensable in a sentence. If there were no subject, there would be nothing to make an assertion about; and if there were no verb, no assertion would be made about the subject. In either case, the group of words would not express a complete thought; that is, it would not be a sentence. Hence in every sentence *the subject and the verb are required*. There are some exceptions to this generalization, as will be explained later, but you will understand sentence structure more easily if you now accept the dogmatic statement that you do not have a sentence unless you have a subject and a verb.

THE DIVISION OF A SENTENCE: SUBJECT AND PREDICATE

8. A sentence may consist entirely of a subject and a verb, as "Birds fly." But in most sentences the subject or the verb or both have modifiers. Consider the following sentences:

> The boy runs down the street.
> The boy in the red sweater runs down the street.
> The boy in the red sweater, who is my cousin, runs swiftly down the street because another boy is chasing him.

In these sentences *boy* is the subject, the substantive about which the assertion is made, and the verb *runs* makes the basic assertion about him. All the other words characterize the boy or describe specifically where, how, and why he runs — that is, all the other words modify the subject or the verb. *Boy* is called the *simple subject;* the words that characterize the boy are called the modifiers of the subject; and the simple subject with its modifiers is called the *complete subject.* In like manner, *runs* is the *simple predicate;* the words that define or expand its meaning are called the modifiers of the predicate; and the simple predicate with its modifiers is called the *complete predicate.*

9. Thought of figuratively, the simple subject and the simple predicate are like two selective magnets, which attract to themselves all words that are appropriate to the statement of a particular complete thought. Notice how the following sentences are made up of two groups, and how the words of each group are attracted to either the simple-subject magnet or the simple-predicate magnet. The groups are separated by a perpendicular line; the simple subject is in italics and the simple predicate in boldface.

> My new *car* | **starts** easily on cold mornings.
> The *tire* that I bought yesterday | **cost** only fifteen dollars.
> The *snow* that fell during the night | **was** soon **melted** by the bright sun.

Subject - actor
Verb - name of action
Object - name - Goal of the action

10. In each of these sentences the subject with its modifiers comes first and the predicate with its modifiers comes second. This is the natural, or normal, order of the words; but when sentences are strung together in a paragraph they frequently deviate from this order. Words of the complete subject and words of the complete predicate are likely to be mixed with one another, and the simple predicate may even precede the simple subject.

> Even on cold mornings my new car starts easily.
> On the top of the hill stands an old stone house.
> Now in swift succession occurred three important events.

THE COMPLEMENT — A BASIC ELEMENT IN THE PREDICATE

11. In the three preceding sentences the simple subject and the simple predicate together convey a complete thought — "Car starts," "House stands," "Events occurred." But consider the following groups of words:

> Yesterday Frank bought.
> Mary made.
> The teacher is.
> He seems.

In each of these the verb obviously does not make a complete assertion about the subject. To complete the sense a third basic element is needed.

> Yesterday Frank bought a new *car*.
> Mary made this *bread*.
> The teacher is my *aunt*.
> He seems *tired*.

The italicized word in each sentence is called the *complement*. The complement is the word or group of words in a sentence that completes the meaning of a verb by stating the recipient or the product of the action or the condition of the subject.

Linking = Copulative
To prove an complement substitute a
form of the verb to be,

12. As a basic element, the complement may be thought of as a third magnet, in addition to the simple subject and the simple predicate, attracting its own modifiers, as in the following sentences:

Alice sent beautiful flowers.
The flowers were big red roses with long stems.
Roses are very pleasing to those who like fragrant flowers.

Nevertheless, since it completes the meaning of a verb, the complement is regarded as a part of the complete predicate and is itself attracted to the magnet of the simple predicate.

13. The kinds of complements will be discussed in detail in Study Unit 7. The illustrative sentences in the preceding paragraph contain the three most common types: *direct object*, *predicate noun*, and *predicate adjective*.

14. The *direct object* is a substantive in the predicate that names the person or thing which receives, or results from, the action of the verb.

The boy next door plays a *saxophone*.
Our neighbor built a new *garage*.

15. The *predicate noun* or *predicate pronoun* is a substantive in the predicate that designates the same person or thing named in the subject; but it does so by using a different substantive from the one used as the subject.

The new play is a gay *comedy*.
The students you asked about are *they*.

16. The *predicate adjective* is an adjective in the predicate that modifies the subject.

The light is *bright*.
The examination was *long*.

17. These three elements — subject, verb, and complement — are basic because they produce the fundamental structure around which the rest of the sentence is built.

The principal elements used to build around them are the modifying and the connective.

Modifying Elements

18. *Modifying elements* are words that limit or make more specific the meaning of other words. Modifiers are either adjectives, which modify substantives, or adverbs, which modify verbs, adjectives, and other adverbs. They may be single words, as already illustrated in Study Unit 1, or groups of words.

> Jockeys ride horses. (No modifiers)
> Those young jockeys ride their fast horses gracefully. (Each of the basic elements has one or more single-word modifiers.)
> Those jockeys *in striped shirts* will ride *when the bell rings*. (The first italicized group of words modifies *jockeys* as if it were a one-word adjective; the second modifies *will ride* as if it were a one-word adverb.)

19. Modifying elements will be discussed in detail in Study Unit 8.

Connective Elements

20. *Connective elements* are words that help to hold together the parts of a sentence and to show the relationship between these parts. The connectives are prepositions, conjunctions, and relative pronouns. You have learned something about their function in Study Units 1 and 2; it will be discussed in greater detail in Study Unit 9.

Appositive Elements

21. An *appositive* is a word or a group of words that helps to identify a person or thing already named by offering another name. It is said to be in apposition with the substantive for which it supplies an alternative desig-

nation.   In each of the following sentences the second italicized word is in apposition with the first.

> *Jones*, our new *gardener*, is young.
> My *brother Fred* made the score.
> Mary was driving her *car*, a new *coupé*, yesterday.
> At last we arrived at our *destination*, a sprawling *village* in a wooded valley.

22. Appositives will be considered further in Study Unit 10.

Independent Elements

23. An *independent element* consists of a word or group of words — even a whole sentence — used within a sentence, but not grammatically related to any word in the sentence. The independent element in each of the following sentences is italicized.

> *Alas*, I cannot come.
> *Fred*, I cannot go tomorrow.
> Used books, *of course*, are less expensive.
> This book, *I have been told*, is exciting.

24. Independent elements will be discussed in detail in Study Unit 11.

An Illustrative Sentence

25. An analysis of the following sentence illustrates how the parts of speech are used as elements in the expression of a thought:

> A wealthy citizen of Farwell, Henry Jones, generously erected this beautiful memorial, you probably recall, after the war ended.

The basic elements of this sentence are:

> *Subject:* citizen
> *Verb:* erected
> *Complement:* memorial

These three words convey the essential thought. All the other words (except the independent element *you probably recall*) help to amplify and clarify the meaning of one or another of these three. Each has a definite relationship to one of the basic elements, some as single words, some in groups functioning as a single word. *Citizen* is clarified by the appositive element, *Henry Jones*, and also by the modifiers *a*, *wealthy*, and *of Farwell;* in the last of these the connective *of* indicates the relationship of *Farwell* to *citizen*. *Erected* is modified by *generously* and by the group *after the war ended*, which is related to the verb by the connective *after*. *Memorial* has attached to it the modifiers *this* and *beautiful*. So in every sentence the basic elements provide a fundamental structure to which the other words (except the independent elements) are related in accordance with their functions.

EXERCISE 4. Identification of Basic Elements and of Words Adhering to Them

In each of the following sentences find the simple basic elements; then state which words adhere to each.

1. From the tall red chimney came white, fluffy smoke.
2. An old mahogany clock stood upon a massive, carved mantel.
3. Large dashing waves beat violently against the cliff.
4. The next batter, a tall, lanky man with unusually long arms, knocked the ball over the fence.
5. Far below us we saw three small lakes, tiny patches of blue water in the green floor of the valley.
6. Eagerly and gracefully his dog, a sleek white greyhound, leaped over the fence.
7. The flood brought a tangled mass of driftwood down the river.
8. The driftwood in the swollen river battered down many buildings.

9. Unexpectedly a strong gust of wind, a miniature tornado, blew our new hats into the street.

10. My Uncle Frank took us to Sandusky, a thriving little city on Lake Erie.

11. An unusually bright flash of lightning blinded us momentarily.

12. The guard on our team, a tall, broad-shouldered young man, intercepted the first pass.

13. In the attic of our house I found a faded daguerreotype, an old picture on tin.

14. A bright, new calendar with large, distinct figures hung conspicuously on the wall.

15. All of the wood in the house was rich, brown mahogany.

16. The bewildered pitcher, a recruit from a minor league, threw the ball over the catcher's head.

17. My cousin Henry took us to the show in his car.

18. Carefully and skillfully they set the big pane of glass in the window.

19. In a small, unfrequented bookstore, a mere box between two tall buildings, he found a rare and valuable book.

20. From the top of the tower we saw the lazy, winding river in the valley, a beautiful and fertile lowland.

Exercise 5.   Identification of Basic Elements and of Words Adhering to Them

Follow the directions for Exercise 4.

In a small semicircular park at the mouth of a cañon in our western mountains, we saw an unusual feat of daring. Here a man walked from the top of one side to the top of the other on a tightrope. At this point the walls were high and straight. Between them stretched a wire cable. To us on the ground it looked like a string. At each end of it was a small platform extending slightly beyond the precipitous face of the wall. Suddenly there was a cheer from the crowd. Then there was a breathless quiet. On one of these platforms appeared a man in tights. All of us watched him closely. Presently he moved out upon the wire. Before him he carried a long pole in order to balance himself. Cautiously he took a short, gliding step. Then he took another and another. Like a mechanical toy he moved slowly toward the middle of the cañon. Here he paused a moment. Then he knelt upon his right knee. Promptly, however, he stood up again and resumed his walk to the other side. From the little platform he waved to us. Relieved from the tensity of the experience, we filled the cañon with our shouts of approval.

Kinds of Sentences

Sentences — a matter of structure

1. Sentences are classified according to the number and the nature of the clauses they contain. By this classification they are called *simple*, *compound*, or *complex*.

2. A *clause* is a group of words that contains a subject and a predicate. In addition, it may contain any or all of the other elements explained in the preceding Study Unit.

3. The kinds of clauses that determine the classification of sentences are known as *independent* and *dependent*.

4. An *independent clause* is capable of standing alone as the expression of a complete thought.

> The service man did not repair our gas stove.

5. A *dependent clause* is a member of another clause, in which it expresses a subordinate thought.

> The service man did not repair our gas stove *because it is too old*. (The italicized words make up the dependent clause.)

Simple Sentence

6. A *simple sentence* consists of one clause, which by itself expresses a complete thought. It never contains another clause. A simple sentence, therefore, is an independent clause; but in general the term *clause* is used in designating a *part* of a sentence.

7. A simple sentence is by no means necessarily a short sentence. Observe the following examples:

Wheels turn.

The red wheel turns rapidly.

The red wheel with the wire spokes turns rapidly.

A solitary, abandoned house with a toppling stone chimney stands on top of a barren hill.

Many shelves of new books with beautifully colored backs lined the walls of the reading room from floor to ceiling.

8. Though a simple sentence has only one subject and one predicate, both or either of them may be compound, as in the following examples:

The *boy* and his *father* went swimming. (Compound subject)

The runner *stumbled* and *fell*. (Compound predicate)

Our *halfback* and the opposing *guard ran* into each other and *fell*. (Compound subject and compound predicate)

Compound Sentence

9. A *compound sentence* consists of two or more independent clauses.

Class A will meet in room 211, and Class B will meet in room 205.

10. Each of these clauses contains a thought that might be expressed separately in a simple sentence, but the writer has combined them because he wishes to indicate a close relationship between them. Both are needed in the sentence to give the writer's full meaning, but neither modifies the other. Each is as important as the other, because each contributes an equally important thought to the total. For this reason the clauses are called *coordinate clauses*.

11. The coordinate clauses in a compound sentence are usually joined by a coordinate conjunction, such as *and, but, or, nor,* and the correlatives *both . . . and, either . . . or, neither . . . nor, not only . . . but also.* Not infrequently, however, the conjunction is omitted.

The wind blew wildly for nearly an hour, and then the rain came down in whipping sheets.

My roommate tried to enter the competition for a scholarship, but his age disqualified him.

Either Fred lost the book on the way home or he left it at the library.

Today the sun is shining; tomorrow we may have rain.

I came, I saw, I conquered.

Complex Sentence

12. When one thought is so subordinate to another that it is a part of the other, the thoughts are expressed in a *complex sentence*. This kind of sentence, like the compound, consists of more than one clause; but it differs from the compound sentence because the clauses are not equal. A complex sentence consists of one independent clause (called the *main clause*) and at least one dependent clause, so called because its meaning depends upon the meaning of the main clause.

13. The manner in which a dependent clause is related to the main clause is shown by a word introducing the dependent clause, usually a subordinate conjunction or a relative pronoun. The types of subordinate connectives will be discussed in Study Unit 9.

14. A dependent clause is so closely related to its main clause that it serves in the main clause as a part of speech, much as a single word would serve. It functions either as a modifier (that is, as an adjective or an adverb) or as a noun.

DEPENDENT CLAUSES USED AS MODIFIERS

15. A dependent clause may be used as an adjective, modifying a substantive, or as an adverb, modifying a verb, an adjective, or an adverb. Compare the following sentences:

The *splintered* tree was blown down last night. (The single word is an adjective modifying *tree*.)

The tree *that the lightning splintered* was blown down last night. (The clause is an adjective modifying *tree*.)

The runners started *tardily*. (The single word is an adverb modifying *started*.)

The runners started *after the official had fired the gun*. (The clause is an adverb modifying *started*.)

DEPENDENT CLAUSES USED AS NOUNS

16. A dependent clause may take the place of a noun in any part of a sentence in which a noun may be used — that is, it may be used as subject, complement, or object of a preposition.

What you said was appropriate. (Subject)

The best part of the discussion was *what you said*. (Predicate noun)

I liked *what you said*. (Object of verb)

He quoted a part of *what you said*. (Object of preposition)

17. The use of dependent clauses as nouns is sometimes confusing because the subordinate nature of the clauses is not so evident as is that of adjective and adverbial clauses, which are modifiers of words in the main clause. These modifying clauses can be omitted without interfering with the grammatical completeness of the main clause, but if a noun clause is omitted the main clause is left grammatically incomplete. Thus a noun clause may seem too essential to be dependent. Nevertheless, it is incapable of standing alone as the expression of a complete thought; its meaning depends upon its relation to the main clause in which it serves as a part of speech.

Compound-Complex Sentence

18. When one or more of the coordinate thoughts in a sentence must be modified by subordinate thoughts, the

whole thought is expressed in a *compound-complex sentence* — that is, a sentence containing two or more independent clauses and one or more dependent clauses.

> Conrad's books, *which you read last summer*, are on the top shelf of the north stack; and Hardy's books are on the bottom shelf of the same stack.
>
> The tall, straight tree *that I always admired* was struck by lightning, but the damage is not noticeable *because the thick foliage hides it.*
>
> Everyone said *that the building was unsafe*, but no one would tell specifically *what was wrong with it.*

Restatement of Definitions

19. A single independent clause forms a *simple sentence.*

> The boys swim every afternoon.

Two or more coordinate clauses form a *compound sentence.*

> The boys play golf in the morning, and they swim in the afternoon.

A main clause and one or more dependent clauses form a *complex sentence.*

> The house was repaired after we moved out.
> The house that we bought is in a suburb where few people live.

Two or more coordinate clauses with one or more dependent clauses form a *compound-complex sentence.*

> We drove to Columbus over the road that went through Jamestown, but we returned by the direct route because we were late

EXERCISE 6. Identification of Kinds of Sentences

Identify each of the following sentences as simple, compound, complex, or compound-complex:

1. The rain began soon after we had pitched our tent.
2. We saw three small sailboats on the river below us.
3. When the cars were loaded, we left for our camp in the mountains.
4. The students and alumni sat in the center section of the grandstand.
5. Since every seat was taken, we had to stand.
6. The boys climbed upon the barge and dived into the water.
7. The first novel that I read was interesting, but its sequel was dull.
8. At camp last summer we followed a carefully planned schedule of activities.
9. From six to seven o'clock in the morning we played tennis, and then we ate breakfast.
10. I could not see who made the touchdown because the people in front of me stood up and obstructed my view.
11. Betty drew all of the illustrations for the yearbook.
12. We floated down the river in a long canoe.
13. Unless the rain stops before noon, we shall not be able to have our picnic.
14. Many small brown sunflowers and white daisies with brown centers grew in the wheat field.
15. If you go to Chicago next summer with your mother, you must visit the art gallery.
16. A limb of the big maple tree cracked in the storm and fell to the ground.
17. The dictionary that was published in 1880 contained many errors, but this revised edition is nearly perfect.
18. At the track meet last Saturday afternoon the hurdlers and pole vaulters made all of our points except two.

19. Every morning before breakfast we ran around the track ten times, and then we took a cool shower.
20. We wondered what was happening at the end of the corridor, where a large group of boys and girls was assembling.

EXERCISE 7.   Identification of Kinds of Sentences

Follow the instructions for Exercise 6.

In a small park that formed a semicircle at the mouth of a cañon in our western mountains, Frank and I saw an unusual performance. Here a man walked a tightrope. This seems like an ordinary feat, but it was not. The walls of the cañon, which consisted of solid rock, were high and straight. Between them, from the top of one to the top of the other, stretched a wire cable, which everybody called a "rope." To us who saw it from the ground it looked like a string. At each end of it was a small platform. On one of these appeared a man in tights. All of us watched him closely. Presently he stepped upon the wire. Before him he carried a long pole, which he moved slightly from side to side. When he seemed to feel sure of himself, he cautiously took a second step, and then he took another. Like a mechanical toy he moved forward until he was nearly an equal distance from each side. Here, in the middle of space, he stopped. Then he knelt upon one knee, rose, and knelt upon the other. Without hesitating, he rose again and resumed his walk to the other side of the cañon. From the little platform he waved to us; and we, recovering from our tense anxiety, filled the cañon with our shouts of approval.

The Verb

Finite — *limits something*
something complete

Primary Function of the ~~Predicate~~ Finite Verb

1. Every sentence must contain a verb which asserts the action of the subject, the action of some agent upon the subject, or the condition of the subject.

> We *enjoyed* his stories. (Action of subject)
> The engineer *was burned* by escaping steam. (Action upon subject)
> The ink *is* purple. (Condition of subject)
> Mother *looks* tired. (Condition of subject)

2. Verbs which assert the condition of the subject, as in the last two sentences in the preceding group, are called *copulative verbs* or *copulas* (that is, linking verbs), because grammatically they link the subject with a predicate noun or a predicate adjective.

3. The most common copulative verb is *be*, with its several forms, such as *am, is, are, was, were, will be, has been*. Other verbs that may be used as copulas are *seem, look, become, appear, prove, grow, sound*.

Verbs.
1. action
2. nonaction

> The building *is* a hotel.
> My uncle *is* tall.
> The answer *seems* correct.
> The bread *looks* fresh.
> The fiddler *became* weary.
> The coat *appears* small.
> The effort *proved* futile.
> The roar of the storm *grew* louder.
> The box *sounds* empty.

a finite a finite verb has a certain tense, voice int time

A non-final verb will depend on the time of the main verb.

4. Many of these verbs, however, may also be used to express the action of the subject or the action of some agent upon the subject.

> I know that I *am*.
> He *looked* for a long time at the picture.
> She *appeared* suddenly in the doorway.
> I *proved* my point without difficulty.
> The point *was proved* by the teacher.
> The child *grew* rapidly.
> This flower *was grown* from seed by Mr. Hamilton.

5. All other predicate verbs assert either the action of the subject or the action of some agent upon the subject, as illustrated by the first two examples in paragraph 1.

Voice

6. The aspect of a verb which indicates whether the subject acts or is acted upon is called *voice*. A verb is said to be in the *active voice* if it expresses an action performed by the subject, and in the *passive voice* if it expresses the action of some agent (which may or may not be named in the sentence) upon the subject. (All copulative verbs are considered active.)

> The ball *hit* the pitcher. (Active)
> The pitcher *was hit* by the ball. (Passive. The agent acting upon the subject is *ball*.)
> Jane *is reading* her new book. (Active)
> This book *has been read* by every member of the class. (Passive. The agent is *member*.)

Transitive and Intransitive Verbs

7. We have already seen that some sentences contain only two basic elements — subject and verb — while others contain a third — the complement. Only copulative verbs are followed by predicate substantives or predi-

cate adjectives. With respect to the other common type of complement, the direct object, verbs are divided into two classes, *transitive* and *intransitive*. A *transitive verb* requires an object to complete its meaning; an *intransitive verb* does not. In other words, a transitive verb (from Latin *transire*, to go across) indicates that the action of the subject goes across it to that which is the result or the recipient of the action — namely, the object; an intransitive verb indicates that the action does not go across to an object. This latter type — with its adverbial modifiers, if needed — states completely all that must be said about the action of the subject, and so an object is not required. Compare, for example, the italicized verbs in the following two sentences:

> The man *writes* a letter.
> The man *writes* rapidly.

In the first sentence the thought is not complete until the object of the action is stated, which is here the result or product instead of the recipient. In the second, there is no result or recipient. The action is merely characterized as being rapid.

8. The foregoing example shows that a single verb may be used both transitively and intransitively. This is true of most verbs, though some are transitive only and some are intransitive only. Some verbs may be used in one sense as transitive verbs and in another as intransitive. Observe the usage in the following sentences:

> Edward plays well.   (Intransitive)
> Edward plays the violin.   (Transitive)
> We danced until midnight.   (Intransitive)
> We danced a quadrille.   (Transitive)
> The flame of the candle burned feebly.   (Intransitive)
> The flame of the candle burned the curtain.   (Transitive)
> The boat floated with the tide.   (Intransitive)
> The salvage crew soon floated the boat.   (Transitive)

Person and Number

9. In addition to expressing the action or condition of the subject, a verb by means of its form serves certain other functions in the sentence.

10. A verb expresses the person and number of its subject.

11. The *person* of a verb shows whether the subject is speaking, is being spoken to, or is being spoken about. There are thus three persons, called *first person*, *second person*, and *third person:*

> I *am going* to the show. (First person)
> You *are going* with me. (Second person)
> The show *is* excellent. (Third person)

12. The *number* of the verb shows whether the subject is *singular* or *plural:*

> I *am going* to the show. (Singular)
> We *are going* to the show. (Plural)
> They *are going* also. (Plural)

13. A verb, therefore, must agree with its subject in person and number.

14. To show this agreement completely, a verb would have to change its form to correspond to each person and number of the subject. In modern English, however, it changes very little. The verb *to be* changes most. All others change only in the third person singular of the present, where they add *s* or *es* (*see, sees; search, searches*), except *have*, which changes to *has*. The following table shows the forms of *be:*

The Verb TO BE

PRESENT TENSE

SINGULAR	PLURAL
I am	We are
You are	You are
He (she, it) is	They are

PAST TENSE

I was	We were
You were	You were
He (she, it) was	They were

Mood

15. A verb expresses also the manner in which the action or condition of the subject is stated. This function of a verb is called *mood*.

16. There are three moods: *indicative*, *imperative*, and *subjunctive*.

INDICATIVE MOOD

17. The indicative mood is used to make a statement that is intended to be positive fact, without condition or uncertainty. The fact may not be true, but the sentence states it as true. Of the three moods, the indicative is the most used.

> The building *is* tall.
> The city *cleaned* our street this morning.
> The Treaty of Vienna *was signed* in 1400. (This is an erroneous statement, but it is made as positive fact.)

18. The indicative mood is used also to ask a direct question that expects a positive answer:

> Who *wrote* this book?
> When *did* Chaucer *die*?

IMPERATIVE MOOD

19. The imperative mood expresses command or request.

> *Close* the door.
> *Be* ready at nine o'clock.
> *Take* the bus at the next corner.

20. The command or request may be made more emphatic by the use of *do*.

> *Do close* the door.
> *Do be* ready at nine o'clock.

21. The subject of a verb in the imperative mood, as these sentences show, is usually not expressed. Inasmuch as the command or request is always addressed to a second person, the subject is assumed to be *you*. As another means of providing emphasis, however, the subject may be used.

> *You* close the door.
> *You* be ready at nine o'clock.

SUBJUNCTIVE MOOD

22. The subjunctive mood is generally used to express a wish, a conditional statement that is doubtful or contrary to fact, or a concession; it also occurs after certain verbs and adjectives expressing command or necessity and after *as if* and *as though*.

> I wish that the superintendent *were* here. (Wish)
> If father *were* here, we could eat our dinner. (Contrary to fact condition)
> If this report *be* true, our work is finished. (Doubtful condition)
> Though it *be* difficult, we must not give up. (Concession)
> I demand that the question *be* reopened. (After verb of commanding)
> It is essential that the culprit *be* caught and punished. (After adjective expressing necessity)
> She walks as if she *were* tired. (After *as if*)

23. The subjunctive mood has been gradually disappearing in modern English. It is still used regularly in poetry and in such formal expression, written or spoken, as legislative enactments, resolutions, exhortations, and

prayers; but in common use it is frequently replaced by the indicative.

> If this report *is* true, our work is finished.
> Though it *is* difficult, it is not impossible.

24. There are only a few forms in which the subjunctive differs from the indicative. The verb *to be* has the form *be* throughout the present subjunctive and the form *were* throughout the past subjunctive. In other verbs, the subjunctive differs from the indicative only in the third person singular of the present tense, where the subjunctive has no final *s*.

Tense

25. A verb also expresses the time of the action or condition of the subject. This aspect of the verb is called *tense*.

> The man *is* here.   (Present)
> The man *was* here.   (Past)
> The man *will be* here.   (Future)

26. Of all the functions of the verb, this is the one that requires the greatest number of changes in form. A verb has six tenses: *present, past, future, present perfect, past perfect*, and *future perfect*. Each of these has different forms in the active voice and in the passive voice.

PRINCIPAL PARTS

27. These tenses are expressed by means of three forms of the verb called principal parts: the present, the past, and the past participle. Note the following examples:

PRESENT	PAST	PAST PARTICIPLE
see	saw	seen
walk	walked	walked

28. These two verbs, you observe, follow two different patterns in forming the past and the past participle. Every verb follows essentially one or the other of these patterns and is classified accordingly as a *strong verb* or a *weak verb*.

29. *Strong verbs*, sometimes called *irregular verbs*, form the past tense by changing the vowel of the present tense; they form the past participle by changing the vowel, by adding *en* or *n*, or by doing both:

PRESENT	PAST	PAST PARTICIPLE
sink	sank	sunk
ride	rode	ridden
rise	rose	risen
sing	sang	sung
know	knew	known
break	broke	broken
grow	grew	grown
freeze	froze	frozen
write	wrote	written

30. *Weak verbs*, sometimes called *regular verbs*, usually form the past tense and the past participle by adding *ed*, *d*, or *t* to the form of the present tense:

PRESENT	PAST	PAST PARTICIPLE
talk	talked	talked
shave	shaved	shaved
plan	planned	planned
fill	filled	filled

31. There are many irregularities in the formation of the principal parts of weak verbs.

Some do not change form in any of the parts: bet, cast, cost, cut, hit, shut, split, thrust.

Some ending in *nd* and *ld* form the past and the past participle by changing the *d* to *t*: bend, bent, bent; lend, lent, lent; build, built, built; etc.

Some with a long vowel shorten the vowel and add *t*: creep, crept, crept; feel, felt, felt; sweep, swept, swept; deal, dealt, dealt; etc.

Some with a long vowel followed by *d* or *t* simply shorten the vowel: feed, fed, fed; speed, sped, sped; meet, met, met; lead, led, led; read, read, read (here the spelling remains the same but the pronunciation changes); etc.

Note also: teach, taught, taught; tell, told, told; seek, sought, sought; think, thought, thought; sell, sold, sold; bring, brought, brought; buy, bought, bought; catch, caught, caught; have, had, had; make, made, made.

In some weak verbs both regular and irregular forms of the past and the past participle occur: dream, dreamed (or dreamt), dreamed (or dreamt); kneel, kneeled, kneeled (or knelt); beseech, beseeched (or besought), beseeched (or besought); light, lighted (or lit), lighted (or lit); etc. Occasionally a verb has both strong and weak forms in the past and the past participle, with differing meanings: shine, shone, shone (intransitive) beside shine, shined, shined (transitive); hang, hung, hung beside hang, hanged, hanged (the latter used of execution by hanging).

32. Three pairs of verbs require your careful study because the principal parts of each pair are frequently confused. These are: *set* (to place), *sit*, *lay*, *lie* (to recline), *raise*, and *rise*. Their principal parts are as follows:

PRESENT	PAST	PAST PARTICIPLE
set	set	set
sit	sat	sat
lay	laid	laid
lie	lay	lain
raise	raised	raised
rise	rose	risen

33. In order to use these verbs properly, you must remember that *set*, *lay*, and *raise* are transitive (that is, they must have a direct object when they are used in the active voice) and that *sit*, *lie*, and *rise* are intransitive. Their correct use is illustrated in the following sentences:

John now *sets* the glass upon the table. (Transitive)
The glass *sits* on the table. (Intransitive)
Mary *lays* the book upon the table. (Transitive)
The book *lies* on the table. (Intransitive)
I *raise* my hand. (Transitive)
I *rise* at five o'clock every morning. (Intransitive)

34. Of course, only the three transitive verbs, *set*, *lay*, and *raise*, are used in the passive.

The pitcher *was set* upon the buffet.
The papers *were laid* upon the table.
The flag *was raised* to the top of the pole.

PRINCIPAL PARTS IN TENSE FORMATION

35. The present and past parts stand alone to express the present active tense and the past active tense respectively. These are the only tenses that can be expressed by means of a single word. Every other tense (and also some special forms of the present and past active tenses) is expressed by combining a form of the verb with a suitable auxiliary.

36. The present part also appears in the future active tense, combined with the auxiliary *shall* or *will*. (On the distinction between them, see below, paragraphs 41–47.)

I *shall send* him.
He *will go*.

37. The past participle never stands alone as a predicate verb, but it is used with various auxiliaries to form a large number of tenses. It is combined with the various forms of *have* to form the three perfect active tenses:

I *have sent*. (Present perfect active)
I *had sent*. (Past perfect active)
I *shall have sent*. (Future perfect active)

It is combined with the various forms of *be* to form all the passive tense forms. Note that the combination of *be* and the past participle is never found in an active tense and is the invariable sign of the passive.

> I *am sent.* (Present passive)
> I *was sent.* (Past passive)
> I *shall be sent.* (Future passive)
> I *have been sent.* (Present perfect passive)
> I *had been sent.* (Past perfect passive)
> I *shall have been sent.* (Future perfect passive)

38. You will notice that the auxiliaries used to form the six tenses are *have* and *be* (with their various forms), *shall*, and *will.* One other auxiliary should be mentioned. *Do* (*did*) is combined with the present part to produce emphatic forms of the present and past tenses and also to express the simple present and past in negative and interrogative sentences:

> I *do hope* that you can come. (Emphatic)
> I *did hope* that he would agree for once. (Emphatic)
> I *do* not *know.* (Negative)
> *Did* you *see* her? (Interrogative)

PRESENT PARTICIPLE IN TENSE FORMATION

39. There is one other form of the verb which, like the past participle, never stands alone as a predicate verb but is combined with auxiliary verbs to form predicate verbs. This is the present participle. Logically it has as good a claim as the past participle to be included among the principal parts; it is omitted because it can be derived readily from the first principal part by the addition of *ing* (sometimes with minor adjustment of spelling): *see, seeing; change, changing; run, running.* As a part of a predicate verb it is combined with various forms of the verb *be* to express continuing or progressive action in all six tenses.

> I *am seeing.* (Present)
> I *was seeing.* (Past)

I *shall be seeing.*   (Future)
I *have been seeing.*   (Present perfect)
I *had been seeing.*   (Past perfect)
I *shall have been seeing.*   (Future perfect)

Passive progressive forms are common only in the present and past. They are formed by combining the progressive forms of *be* with the past participle.

I *am being seen.*
I *was being seen.*

Auxiliary Verbs

40. To form the tenses that have been discussed, the auxiliaries needed are *shall* and *will*, *be*, *have*, and *do*, in their various forms. The first two require special consideration.

SHALL AND WILL, SHOULD AND WOULD

41. The modern tendency is to distinguish less carefully than formerly between *shall* and *will;* but certain distinctions are still observed by careful writers.

42. To express simple futurity, *shall* is used with the first person and *will* with the second and third.

I shall go with you tomorrow.
You will soon own all of George Eliot's novels.
John will sing tomorrow.

43. To express determination or promise on the part of the speaker, the usage is exactly reversed: *will* is used with the first person and *shall* with the second and third.

I will go with you whether you want me or not.
I will be here tomorrow at two, rain or shine.
You shall go; I have set my heart upon it.
Bob shall walk to school despite his protests.

44. To express determination or promise on the part of the person spoken of, *will* is used in both the second and third persons.

> You will go despite all I can say. (You are determined to go.)
>
> Bob will walk to school in spite of my protests. (Bob is determined to walk.)

45. In interrogative sentences, the form that is expected in the answer is used.

> Shall I go tomorrow?
>
> Shall you be here when I get back? (Expected answer: *I shall* or *I shall not;* simple futurity.)
>
> Will you go on with this thing in spite of everything your friends can do? (Expected answer: *I will* or *I will not;* determination or promise.)

46. In indirect discourse, the form that would be correct in the corresponding direct discourse is used. (Other subordinate clauses follow the same rules as main clauses.)

> Father says that he shall not come home for lunch. (Father says: "I shall not come home for lunch.")

47. In general, the same distinctions hold for *should* and *would*. Remember that in indirect discourse after a verb in the past, *should* and *would* regularly correspond to *shall* and *will* in direct discourse. Study the usage in the following sentences:

> I should have a good time if I went, but I certainly would not go without you.
>
> You would have a good time if you went, but you certainly would not go without me.
>
> Should you like to go?
>
> He said that he should not be back for lunch.
>
> He said that he would certainly not try again.

MODAL AUXILIARIES

48. In addition to the auxiliaries discussed above, by means of which the various tenses are formed, certain other auxiliaries are used to form verb phrases that express permission, possibility, obligation, necessity, etc. They are *may* (*might*), *can* (*could*), *must*, and also *would* and *should* in some senses. These words are called modal auxiliaries. The following sentences give some examples of their use:

> You may come at nine. (**P**ermission)
> You may find him there. (Possibility)
> I could see you tomorrow. (Ability)
> You must do it yourself. (Necessity)
> You should go to bed early. (Obligation)
> He would go there day after day. (Habitual action)

Conjugation of Typical Verbs

49. The following table gives the forms for the six tenses in the indicative mood. (For the few forms in which the subjunctive differs from the indicative see paragraph 24, above.)

The Verb TO BE

PRESENT TENSE

SINGULAR	PLURAL
I am	We are
You are	You are
He is	They are

PAST TENSE

I was	We were
You were	You were
He was	They were

FUTURE TENSE

SINGULAR	PLURAL
I shall be	We shall be
You will be	You will be
He will be	They will be

PRESENT PERFECT TENSE

I have been	We have been
You have been	You have been
He has been	They have been

PAST PERFECT TENSE

I had been	We had been
You had been	You had been
He had been	They had been

FUTURE PERFECT TENSE

I shall have been	We shall have been
You will have been	You will have been
He will have been	They will have been

The Verb TO SEE

ACTIVE VOICE

PRESENT TENSE

SINGULAR	PLURAL
I see	We see
You see	You see
He sees	They see

PAST TENSE

I saw	We saw
You saw	You saw
He saw	They saw

FUTURE TENSE

I shall see	We shall see
You will see	You will see
He will see	They will see

PRESENT PERFECT TENSE

SINGULAR	PLURAL
I have seen	We have seen
You have seen	You have seen
He has seen	They have seen

PAST PERFECT TENSE

I had seen	We had seen
You had seen	You had seen
He had seen	They had seen

FUTURE PERFECT TENSE

I shall have seen	We shall have seen
You will have seen	You will have seen
He will have seen	They will have seen

PASSIVE VOICE

PRESENT TENSE

SINGULAR	PLURAL
I am seen	We are seen
You are seen	You are seen
He is seen	They are seen

PAST TENSE

I was seen	We were seen
You were seen	You were seen
He was seen	They were seen

FUTURE TENSE

I shall be seen	We shall be seen
You will be seen	You will be seen
He will be seen	They will be seen

PRESENT PERFECT TENSE

I have been seen	We have been seen
You have been seen	You have been seen
He has been seen	They have been seen

PAST PERFECT TENSE

SINGULAR	PLURAL
I had been seen	We had been seen
You had been seen	You had been seen
He had been seen	They had been seen

FUTURE PERFECT TENSE

I shall have been seen	We shall have been seen
You will have been seen	You will have been seen
He will have been seen	They will have been seen

Verbals are not finite verbs.

50. Up to this point we have been discussing predicate verbs — that is, verbs that can by themselves make an assertion about the subject. There are certain other forms of the verb that cannot serve this function. They are called *verbals*, and they are of three kinds: *participles*, *gerunds*, and *infinitives*. Their distinguishing — and also confusing — characteristic is that, in addition to having some of the properties of verbs, each serves also as another part of speech.

PARTICIPLE

51. A *participle* is both a verb and an adjective.
52. It has several forms, as follows:

	ACTIVE	PASSIVE
PRESENT:	seeing	being seen
PAST:		seen
PERFECT:	having seen	having been seen

53. The following sentence illustrates the double function of the participle:

The *burning* oil well illuminated the sky.

As a form of the verb, *burning* indicates the action or condition of the oil well, but it does not make the main assertion about it. As an adjective it modifies *well*.

54. Since a participle functions as an adjective, it must always modify a substantive. But since it is also a form of the verb, it may, like any verb, have a complement and adverbial modifiers.

> The oil well, *burning* like a huge candle, illuminated the sky. (*Burning* as an adjective modifies *well*, but as a verb it is itself modified by an adverbial phrase.)
> The oil well, *illuminating* the sky for miles around, burned all night. (*Illuminating* modifies *well*, but it also has a direct object and an adverbial modifier.)

55. The participle and all the words related to it in its function as a verb, such as object and modifiers, constitute a participial phrase. *Illuminating the sky for miles around* in the preceding sentence, for example, is a participial phrase. Participial phrases will be treated in detail in Study Unit 14.

GERUND

56. A *gerund* is both a verb and a noun.

57. A gerund has exactly the same form as a participle; you can distinguish the two only by their use. By far the most frequent form of the gerund is the present active, ending in *ing*.

58. As a verb, a gerund (like a participle) can have a complement and adverbial modifiers. As a noun, it may be used wherever a noun may be used; that is, it may be a subject, a predicate noun, an object of a verb or a preposition, or an appositive.

> *Fishing* is the most peaceful recreation. (Subject)
> The most peaceful recreation is *fishing*. (Predicate noun)
> I recommend *fishing* as a peaceful recreation. (Direct object)
> The most exciting kind of *fishing* is in a mountain brook. (Object of preposition)
> My favorite sport, *fishing*, has many devotees. (Appositive)

59. A gerund and all the words related to it in its function as a verb and as a noun constitute a gerund phrase.

> *Fishing for trout in a mountain brook* is exciting.
> *Planning the campaign carefully* will produce good results.

Gerund phrases will be treated in detail in Study Unit 14.

INFINITIVE

60. An *infinitive* is a verb and also a noun, an adjective, or an adverb.

61. It has the following forms:

	ACTIVE	PASSIVE
PRESENT:	to see	to be seen
PERFECT:	to have seen	to have been seen

62. The following sentences illustrate the use of the infinitive as noun, adjective, and adverb:

> *To run* is easy.   (Noun, serving as the subject of the sentence)
> He had a strong desire *to leave*.   (Adjective, modifying the noun *desire*)
> His method is sure *to succeed*.   (Adverb, modifying the adjective *sure*)

63. Like the other verbals, an infinitive may have a complement and adverbial modifiers.   An infinitive and the words related to it in its function as a verb constitute an infinitive phrase.

> *To run from danger when no one is watching* is easy.
> You should learn *to sing the song more vigorously*.

Infinitive phrases will be treated in detail in Study Unit 15.

LIMITATION AS VERBS

64. Remember that verbals, though they are forms of a verb, are used primarily as other parts of speech.   They are not predicate verbs, though certain forms of the infinitive and the participle, combined with suitable auxiliaries, form verb phrases that are predicate verbs.

EXERCISE 8.   Principal Parts of Verbs— *basic form*

Each form given below is one of the three principal parts of a verb. State which part it is, and then give the other two parts.

rise	sat	know	begin	raise
lain	do	set	speak	came
see	drink	ride	throw	drag
go	eat	take	ring	run
laid	gave	write	blow	broke
bitten	dive	flown	fall	chose
get	sprang	pay	left	flow
shook	stay	swim	wake	build

EXERCISE 9.   Principal Parts of Verbs

Use each of the following principal parts of verbs correctly as a predicate verb in a sentence. If the principal part cannot be used alone as a predicate verb, supply a suitable auxiliary, but not otherwise.

gave	set	lay (*reclined*)	raise
went	rose	ran	wrote
drank	took	began	broke
laid	spoke	did	saw
eat	rang	lain	sit

EXERCISE 10.   Principal Parts of Verbs

Use each of the three principal parts of the following verbs correctly as the predicate verb of a sentence. When the principal part requires an auxiliary verb, state which is the principal part and which is the auxiliary.

sit	lie (*to recline*)	rise
set (*to place*)	lay	raise

EXERCISE 11. Principal Parts and Tenses of Verbs

Supply the specified form of the verb.

1. Last year our classes (*begin: past*) a day earlier.
2. We frequently (*dive: present perfect*) from that pier.
3. The boys (*fly: present perfect*) their kite every day.
4. Joe (*set: past*) the lamp upon the table.
5. He (*blow: past*) into the clarinet, but it never made a sound.
6. At the intermission the players (*lie: past*) on the field to rest.
7. When the assignment was made, I already (*write: past perfect*) my theme.
8. The big electric sign (*swing: past*) in the wind.
9. The wind (*blow: present perfect*) for two days.
10. Those two dogs (*eat: past*) all the fish that we caught.
11. The gasoline from the broken pump (*flow: present perfect*) over the sidewalk.
12. Coming down a long winding road, we (*see: past*) a herd of deer grazing at the bottom of the hill.
13. Yesterday John (*run: past*) a hundred yards in ten seconds.
14. A slight quake this morning (*shake: past*) nearly every house in town.
15. The children (*sing: past*) carols last night.
16. The clock (*sat: present*) on the table.
17. The flag (*rise: past*) slowly to the top of the pole.
18. The catcher quickly (*throw: past*) the ball to the first baseman.

19. After our long hike, we (*sleep: past*) soundly.

20. The fire bell (*ring: past*) twice in one evening.

21. Fred (*sat: present*) in that big leather chair.

22. Yesterday I (*swim: past*) the length of the pool.

23. The postman (*take: present perfect*) the letters.

24. We (*bring: present perfect*) our music.

25. The cat (*drink: present perfect*) all of the cream.

26. The bootblack (*shine: present perfect*) our shoes.

27. All of the boys (*go: present perfect*) to the circus.

28. The dog (*lain: present*) on the chair.

29. John (*swim: present perfect*) across the river.

30. Betty (*see: present perfect*) this show twice.

31. The curtain (*rise: past perfect*) five minutes before we arrived.

32. The principal (*ring: present perfect*) the bell for fire drill.

33. The bear (*eat: present perfect*) all of our bacon.

34. I (*do: past*) my work as soon as I was told.

35. We (*sit: present perfect*) here for an hour waiting for you.

36. Sheets of paper (*lain: past*) on the floor.

37. John (*throw: present perfect*) the ball over the fence.

38. The little girl (*drag: present perfect*) her coat through the mud.

39. Your book (*lie: present perfect*) on this table all week.

40. The sun (*shine: present perfect*) bright since noon.

41. Alice (*set: present perfect*) the bowl of flowers on the table.

42. Doris now (*lay: present*) her doll upon the bed.

43. The wind (*shake: present perfect*) the clock off the mantle.

44. Fred (*ride: past*) with us to Cleveland.

45. Tom (*lay: present perfect*) the magazine upon the table.

46. The powerful crane easily (*raise: past*) the big ladle of molten steel.

47. Someone (*lay: present perfect*) this magazine upon my desk.

48. I (*ride: present perfect*) my horse every afternoon this week.

49. The wind (*begin: present perfect*) to blow.

50. This clock (*run: present perfect*) continuously for five years.

EXERCISE 12.   Principal Parts of Verbs
as Complete Predicate Verbs

Point out the predicate verbs in the following sentences
and state the tense of each.

1. The road was narrow and steep.
2. We drove up the road in high gear.
3. The engine was laboring before we reached the top.
4. We had never driven over this road until yesterday.
5. On top of the road was a small park.
6. In the middle of the park stood an observation tower.
7. This tower had been erected in 1898.
8. It marked the site of some famous battle in the Indian wars.
9. We stopped our car at the base of a long wooden stairway.
10. It was old and rickety.
11. Being dared by a member of the group, we decided to climb to the top.
12. Most of us were sorry before we had gone halfway.
13. In climbing to the top we counted one hundred and ten steps.
14. When we reached the top, we saw a beautiful valley.
15. In the foreground we saw rows and rows of cherry trees.
16. We were told that these trees had been blooming only the week before.
17. We were sorry that we had not seen them.
18. Beyond the orchard were acres of wheat waving in the breeze.
19. On either side of the orchard was a field of young corn planted in long, straight rows.
20. Along the outer edge of these fields, looking like giant guards, stood many clusters of tall, straight trees, shaking their heads as the wind blew over them.

Exercise 13. Principal Parts of Verbs as Complete Predicate Verbs

Point out all the predicate verbs in the following sentences and state the tense of each.

The largest crowd of the season was waiting tensely for the opening of the championship football game. Nearly every student, hundreds of townspeople, and visitors from all parts of the state were there. The most eager and the most demonstrative of all, of course, were the students. In the center section of the grandstand they were seated in "yelling formation." On the front seats was a group of about fifty young men in red and white striped coats. Apparently they were chosen for their special ability to make noise. Behind this group were sitting other young men without uniforms. Many of them, however, wore gaily colored sweaters and caps. With this group most of the young men of the student body had been seated. On either side of these men was a section or two of girls. Down upon the ground in front of the men's section were prancing three young men in light-blue flannel coats and white trousers. Each one was holding a large megaphone. The young man in the center had raised his megaphone to his mouth. Few people except those in front of him heard his remarks. Apparently, though, he was giving instructions. Throwing his trumpet to the ground, he stretched his arms high above his head. Simultaneously the entire group of students rose and yelled lustily. All three young men now had thrown aside their megaphones, and, with their arms upstretched, they were weaving their bodies rhythmically from side to side. Suddenly they stood still, and the students became silent and sat down. Within a few minutes, however, someone called out, "Here they come!" Immediately everyone stood and shouted independently, and the three young men with megaphones danced and jumped and turned somersaults. What had happened? Everyone knows, of course. The home team was trotting down the center of the field.

EXERCISE 14. *Shall* and *Will;* *Should* and *Would*

Choose the proper form for each sentence and explain your choice.

1. Classes (shall, will) begin Monday at eight o'clock.
2. If we had the proper clothes, we (should, would) climb the mountain.
3. Climbing that mountain is dangerous. You (shall, will) not go.
4. Bob said that he (should, would) go if he could.
5. (Shall, Will) you take a history course this year?
6. I certainly (should, would) not ride in that old airplane.
7. They said that they (should, would) come tomorrow.
8. We have stipulated in the contract that the bus (shall, will) leave the depot promptly at nine o'clock.
9. Mary and Jane say that they (shall, will) be late to the meeting.
10. The chairman knows that I (shall, will) be absent.

EXERCISE 15. Identification of Verbals

Identify each participle, gerund, and infinitive in the following sentences:

1. Reading as fast as I could for several hours each day, I finished the book in one week.
2. On one corner of the house was a large cone with a weather vane rising several feet from its tip.
3. I expect to climb to the top of the mountain.
4. Because the road was too rough for anyone to drive over it, the guard asked us to take another road farther south.
5. To light the streets of a city properly is expensive.
6. The road became narrower and steeper as we approached

the top of the hill, but we continued to go forward because
we saw no place to turn around.

7. Having read all of one evening about the bleak <u>country</u>
<u>described</u> in *Wuthering Heights*, I was too fascinated to
move.

8. Standing five hundred feet above its nearest neighbor,
the white peak of the mountain glistened in the bright
sunshine.

9. The fog, hanging low in the valley as we drove over the
top of the hill, was like a billowy sea.

10. Traveling in the hot summer months exhausts even those
people who live regularly in warm climates.

11. Yesterday I read a book that told about the author's experiences in riding a bicycle from Berlin to Paris.

12. By taking the road through Stratton we saved an hour's
time.

13. Diving in shallow water is dangerous for anyone who is
not an expert swimmer.

14. As he tilted his chair, it slipped on the freshly oiled floor,
throwing him against the wall so hard that he fractured
his skull.

15. He tried to balance himself as he crept over the log
spanning the creek, but he wobbled so much that he
slipped and fell into the chilly water.

16. On the building were four large pillars to support the
dome.

17. Over the windows in that old log house, built in 1815, were
sheets of paper dipped in oil.

18. A large black cloud came up the narrow valley, changing
bright day into dusk.

19. Disheartened and alone, the old man sat day after day
in his cabin, reading the few books that he owned.

20. The legend is that an old hermit, knowing that his end
was about to come, climbed into the high cave yonder
and died.

The Subject

1. The subject of a sentence or clause names the person or thing about which the verb makes an assertion. Since its function is to name, a subject must be a noun or a substitute for a noun. In other words, a subject must be a substantive.

2. If you are in doubt about what the subject of a sentence is or whether your own sentence contains a subject, you should first discover the verb and then ask *who* or *what* of the verb. Take the following sentences as examples:

> The engineer inspects the turbines.
> The engines in the powerhouse are tall.

In the first sentence the verb is *inspects*. Who inspects? The engineer. *Engineer*, then, is the subject. In the second sentence the verb is *are*. What possesses the state or condition expressed by the verb? Engines.

Position of Subject

3. When the parts of a sentence are in their natural order, the subject comes first. The simple subject, of course, is often preceded by its adjective modifiers, but the complete subject heads the sentence. In the following sentences the complete subject is followed by an oblique line.

> He/turned around slowly.
> Our team/made two touchdowns in the first five minutes
> of the last quarter.

> A careful driver/decelerates his car cautiously when he
> stops on an icy street.
> Three large old elm trees/stood in the center of the park.

4. Often, however, some parts must be out of their
natural order — in what is called inverted order, with
the subject preceded by one or more adverbial modifiers
of the verb (which may be words, phrases, or clauses) or
even by the entire predicate.   Observe the following rewriting of the foregoing sentences:

> Slowly he turned around.
> In the first five minutes of the last quarter, our team made
> two touchdowns.
> When he stops on an icy street, a careful driver decelerates
> his car cautiously.
> In the center of the park stood three large old elm trees.

5. Inverted order is necessary for the following reasons:
  a. To gain emphasis.
  b. To provide smooth coherence between the parts of
a sentence, or between sentences.
  c. To relieve the monotony of similar sentence structure within a paragraph.

Types of Substantive Used as Subject

6. Since many persons write monotonous sentences
merely because they do not know what types of words
may be used as subjects of sentences, you should carefully go over the classification in the following paragraph.

7. The subject of a sentence may be a *noun*, a *pronoun*,
a *gerund* or a *gerund phrase*, an *infinitive* or an *infinitive
phrase*, or a *clause*.

NOUN AS SUBJECT

8. Few students have any difficulty in recognizing single
nouns as subjects.

The *earth* revolves on its axis.

The *paper* is too highly glazed.

A *desk* and a *chair* are in each room. (Compound subject)

The *deans, instructors,* and *students* attended the convocation. (Compound subject)

Nor do many fail to recognize as subject a group of related words functioning as a single noun. A group of this kind, as used in the following sentences, is sometimes called a *noun phrase.*

J. P. Wildy and Sons sold us our new tractor.

The *Encyclopaedia Britannica* is published in twenty-four volumes.

PRONOUN AS SUBJECT

9. Many students, however, are perplexed about the use of the pronoun as subject. The second of the two following sentences is an illustration:

The books are on the table. They have not been used.

Some students recall, quite properly, that a group of words is not a sentence unless it can stand alone. Since *they* is not clear without *books*, these students conclude that *they* is not a subject and hence that the second group of words is not a sentence. What they fail to recall is that a sentence must be *grammatically* independent, not necessarily *logically* independent. It is true that *they* has a vague meaning when it is isolated from its antecedent, but grammatically it is a substantive capable of serving as the subject of a sentence. *They have not been used* is a grammatically complete sentence because it contains a subject and a predicate and is not subordinated to another thought.

10. Personal, indefinite, interrogative, and demonstrative pronouns can all function as subjects.

11. *Personal Pronouns*

He made the first score.
We attended the concert.
You will be on time if you hurry.

12. *Indefinite Pronouns*

Both of us are going to the game.
Another has been chosen captain.
Several came in for a game of table tennis.

13. *Interrogative Pronouns*

Who is going with us?
Which is my book?
What is coming down the street?

14. *Demonstrative Pronouns*

This is my pencil.
That is your pen.
These came from the apple tree in our back yard.

15. Caution 1. Remember that indefinites, interrogatives, and demonstratives may be used as adjectives as well as pronouns, and that when they are used as adjectives they cannot, of course, function as subjects.

16. Caution 2. Do not be too hasty about construing the pronouns *who*, *which*, *what* at the beginning of sentences as subjects. They may have different functions, as the following sentences (in which the subjects are italicized) illustrate:

Which shall *I* give you? (Object of verb)
What are *you* thinking of? (Object of preposition)
Who made this violin is not known. (Subject of noun clause, which is the subject of the sentence)
Who made this violin *we* do not know. (Subject of noun clause, which is the object of the verb)

What the man said is not known.   (Object of noun clause, which is the subject of the sentence)

What the man said *we* never discovered.   (Object of noun clause, which is the object of the verb)

GERUND OR GERUND PHRASE AS SUBJECT

17. Since a gerund is a verbal used as a noun it may be the subject of a sentence, as in the following examples:

Skating is invigorating.

Swimming was his chief accomplishment.

Running is dangerous for anyone with a bad heart.

18. When the gerund-subject has modifiers or other words related to it, such as adjectives, objects, or a predicate noun, it and its related words — called a *gerund phrase* — are the subject, as in the following examples:

Skating every day in the crisp December air made our complexions ruddy.

Swimming the English Channel is a feat not undertaken by many.

Running a mile each day in both good and bad weather developed Jack's heart and lungs.

19. CAUTION. Since a gerund and a present participle look exactly alike, you must be sure that you do not mistake a participle for a gerund-subject, especially when the participle or participial phrase comes at the beginning of a sentence, as it does in the following illustrations:

Skating on thin ice around the edge of the lake, we avoided the large crowd in the center.

Swimming slowly beside a canoe, he crossed the river in twenty-five minutes.

Running awkwardly over the rough field, the young colt followed his mother to the corral.

INFINITIVE OR INFINITIVE PHRASE AS SUBJECT

20. Since an infinitive is a verbal that may have the function of a noun, as well as that of an adjective and an adverb, it may be the subject of a sentence, as in the following sentences:

> *To skate* is his sole ambition.
> *To swim* is to risk one's life.
> *To run* is to admit that we are afraid.

21. When the infinitive subject has modifiers or other words related to it, such as an object, it and its related words — called an *infinitive phrase* — are the subject, as in the following examples:

> *To skate up the river from Greensburg to Russellville* is his one ambition.
> *To swim in this boisterous lake* requires skill and endurance.
> *To run from here now* is to admit that we are afraid.
> *For us to climb the peak now* would be dangerous. (This is a peculiar infinitive phrase in which *us* is said to be the subject of the infinitive *to climb*. This type of phrase is often introduced by *for*. Strictly construed, the whole infinitive phrase is the object of the preposition *for*. Thus the subject of the sentence is really a prepositional phrase, though the important part is the infinitive. The whole phrase serves as a noun, much as if it were a gerund phrase: *Our climbing the peak now* would be dangerous.)

CLAUSE AS SUBJECT

22. A noun clause may be the subject of a sentence.
23. A noun clause may be introduced by any of the following connectives: *that, whether (whether . . . or), who (whoever), which (whichever), what (whatever), why, when, where, how, whence,* and *whither.* Some of these connectives can also introduce adverbial clauses; but such clauses must modify verbs or adjectives and so they ob-

viously cannot be subjects. The use of these connectives in noun clauses as subjects is illustrated in the following sentences:

> *That our team played a better game* was admitted by everyone.
>
> *Whether the band will march in the parade* has not been decided.
>
> *Who is the queen in the May Day celebration* is a secret.
>
> *Which is mine* depends upon your choice.
>
> *What caused the fire* was never known.
>
> *Why we could not go* was not explained.
>
> *Where we are going* is not for you to know.
>
> *How we shall earn enough money for our trip* is a problem that we have not yet solved.

24. CAUTION. Often a noun clause at the head of a sentence is not a subject, but an object out of its normal order, as in the following illustrations:

> *Who is to be the queen in the May Day celebration*, the committee will announce tomorrow.
>
> *Which is mine*, I leave for you to decide.
>
> *Why we could not go with him*, the guide did not explain.
>
> *Where we are going*, you are not supposed to know.
>
> *How we shall earn enough money for our trip*, we have not yet decided.

Omission of Subject

25. On the regular omission of the subject in imperative sentences, see Study Unit 5, paragraph 21.

EXERCISE 16. Subjects of Sentences

Identify the substantive that is the *simple subject* of each of the following sentences. Remember that a substantive may be a noun, a pronoun, a gerund or gerund phrase, an infinitive or infinitive phrase, or a clause.

1. The men wearing the blue shirts scaled the steep side of the mountain.
2. This is the contribution that our class is making to the library.
3. To decorate all of the tables for the junior-senior banquet was our assignment.
4. Which picture was the best, the critics could not decide.
5. This is the book that I read last week.
6. That Frank and Anne ought to lead the grand march is the opinion of everyone.
7. They drove over the mountain pass in a blinding snow-storm.
8. Where I lost my pen, I do not know.
9. Whoever sells ten tickets will be given one complimentary ticket.
10. What witty and clever remarks did he make in his speech last night?
11. You must complete all three parts of this test within one hour.
12. Whatever the committee decides about the program will be approved by the class.
13. Whom we ask to our party is for us to decide.
14. Whither the stranger went was a question that no one could answer.
15. That is a new book for the public library.
16. That the book was written after 1800 is shown by a reference on page 18 of Charles Dickens' *Pickwick Papers*.
17. To take part in this program you must learn these two speeches.
18. He informed me yesterday that his team will not be able to play next Saturday.
19. The Frank C. Walker Company of Newton, Ohio, made the uniforms for our band.
20. Running increases one's chest expansion.
21. Running around his opponent's right end, the halfback made a touchdown.
22. When the audience applauded for an encore, both came out and merely bowed.

23. How the story ended, we were eager to know.
24. To conserve his energy in the beginning of a race is the hardest lesson that a long-distance runner has to learn.
25. His last quick and accurate pass to the right end won the game.
26. That Esther had studied faithfully was shown by the results of her examination.
27. Whether the team wins or not is less important than the kind of game that it plays.
28. Both of them are interesting books.
29. Why classes were excused, no one knows.
30. What the newspaper said about the excellent rebuttal of our debating team was admitted even by the opponents.
31. To have every actor on the stage in time for his cue was no small task.
32. That the wind was blowing we could tell by the puffs of smoke coming into the room from the fireplace.
33. How the magician did the trick was not guessed by anyone.
34. Which of these violins do you intend to buy?
35. Why the penalty had been imposed was asked by everyone.
36. What happened to my pen?
37. Who has been chosen to play the leading role?
38. By checking our list we found that two members had not paid their dues.
39. My brother, whom you met at the lecture last Saturday, will leave next week for Detroit.
40. That house on the hill was built five years after this town was first settled.
41. Who attended the dance last night was not reported in the paper.
42. That clock is one hour slow.
43. His quick thinking when he discovered a small fire in the basement saved the house from burning.
44. Which is the pen that you chose?
45. Ours is not so new as yours because it had been used six months when we bought it.

46. When the first touchdown was made, a group of students set off a big bomb.

47. Those are my pictures.

48. What Jim was paid for his work was more than he had expected.

49. Some did not like the music that we played at the dance last night.

50. Several members of our class won scholarships.

EXERCISE 17. Subjects of Sentences

Group the words into grammatically complete sentences and state the kind of punctuation mark that should be used at the end of each sentence. Remember that a complete sentence may be simple, compound, or complex. Next, point out the substantive that is the *simple subject* of each simple sentence, each coordinate clause of a compound sentence, and each main clause of a complex sentence.

Why everything went wrong when we tried to prepare our first supper I do not know the reason probably was that none of us had camped in the mountains of the five of us no one had even been in the mountains except Melvin when he was a boy an uncle had taken him on a sightseeing trip through Yellowstone Park with a party of tourists because he had had this experience he felt superior to the rest of us until he upset our bucket of coffee and nearly put out the fire how he felt after that accident was his own secret we knew only that he suddenly became unusually quiet and humble he had completely dethroned himself from his assumed leadership in his place however rose one of us who had had the least experience this was Charlie he had never seen a mountain before this trip but he had enough practical sense to know how to build a fireplace on which we could cook our supper the rest of us never pretended to know anything we were merely followers probably I am giving you the impression that our recreation had always been limited to the playing of billiards and ping-pong and similar indoor sports if I am I am misleading you all of us were accustomed to outdoor life but we had always been gentleman campers who after having fished all day returned to a comfortable cabin on the bank of the river where we had stoves and firewood and beds in the mountains we were gypsies fishing a while in one stream and then driving to another when night came we pitched camp wherever we happened to be after we had had some experience we knew what to do but on the first night we bungled everything

Preparing a camp supper is not difficult but for us it was exasperating we were so awkward that we nearly ruined all of our food our fire for instance would not heat our skillet and coffee bucket though it was hot enough to burn everything around it including us building the fire was my task I must therefore take full responsibility for the failure what I decided was that we needed a big fire why I did not know better still puzzles me though I now think that I see at least one explanation the trouble was that I had never built this kind of fire what similar fires I had built were always big camp fires these were supposed to be bright and cheerful in building this fire therefore I followed my usual practice everyone in the group furthermore seemed to agree that I was proceeding properly I was even somewhat proud of myself to provide something on which we could place a grill for our utensils I carefully made four pillars of rocks these were about two feet high and two feet apart upon these pillars I placed the grill which fortunately was large enough to fit why should I not have been well pleased with myself I had built a substantial and convenient fireplace with a top large enough for both our skillet and coffee bucket the fire moreover burned lustily it roared to have a fire however is one thing but to direct the heat is quite another what I discovered was that this hot fire of mine was not providing heat where I wanted it a strong west breeze in fact was blowing the flames so that they did not even touch the grill what could I do I felt helpless Charlie was all ready to fry our bacon and eggs but the skillet would not get hot Melvin thought that he could help by piling rocks on the east side of the fireplace the darting flames however excited him so much that he dropped a large rock into the fire this flipped a burning stick upon the greasy paper that contained the bacon at once it was ablaze reaching into this new fire with a stick Charlie tried to pull out the bacon but he merely scattered it all of it burned except a few pieces that he had raked into the sand these we were able to wash and use in the excitement however Bob had stepped into a carton of eggs and Melvin had toppled over a pillar of the fireplace how he did it is not yet clear but he knocked it over the grill tilted and the bucket of coffee spilled into the fire the sizzling and sputtering merely added to our confusion jumping from one accident into another we must have looked ridiculous P. T. Barnum undoubtedly would have engaged us for his side show if he had seen us who can be more amusing than a full-grown person so flustered that he does not know what he is doing I was that kind of person I do not deny it everyone in the group furthermore was that kind all of them admitted that they were Charlie however was the first to recover his senses he usually was his practical mind generally got us out of our difficulties while the rest of us were now trying futilely to mend what had been ruined he built a new fireplace this one was properly constructed it was small and low with only one side open why I did not think of this kind I do not know anyone could see at once that he had followed the right principle what he did with his small oven was to concentrate the heat what I did was to scatter it cooking on his fireplace therefore was easy the reason was that the heat was forced against our cooking utensils because of this concentration they became hot almost as quickly as if they had been on a gas burner when we fully realized that we had a serviceable fire we soon got together a fresh supply of food and began to prepare it our despair was turned into hope that we now should have supper in spite of our mishaps was certain

The Complement

1. Every sentence, except a few special kinds explained later, must have at least two basic elements — a subject and a verb; but some thoughts cannot be expressed without a third basic element. It is needed when the complete expression of the action or condition indicated by the the verb requires a word or a group of words designating recipient or the result of the action of the subject or the condition of the subject. This word or group of words is called the *complement*.

2. These functions of the complement are illustrated in the following sentences:

> The whole class read the wrong *chapter*.
> Mr. Smith wrote this *chapter*.
> A chapter is a *unit* of a book.
> The chapter is much too *long*.

3. There are three classes of complements: *objects*, *predicate nouns*, and *predicate adjectives*.

Objects

4. Objects that serve as complements of verbs are *direct objects*, *indirect objects*, *predicate objectives*, and *cognate objects*.

DIRECT OBJECT

5. The *direct object* is the most frequently used of these four. It is a substantive that denotes whatever receives the action of a verb or is produced by it. Since the order of basic elements in the development of a thought is sub-

ject, verb, and complement, you can identify a direct
object by inserting the simple question "What?" or
"Whom?" *after* the verb.

>A rock broke the windshield. (Broke *what?*)
>The rock hit the driver. (Hit *whom?*)

6. A direct object may be any of the several kinds of
substantive, namely, *noun, pronoun, gerund* or *gerund
phrase, infinitive* or *infinitive phrase,* or *noun clause:*

>He opened the *door* quietly. (Noun)
>We saw *him* at the door. (Pronoun)
>We heard the *shouting.* (Gerund)
>They enjoyed *reading the book.* (Gerund phrase)
>Charlotte wants *to go.* (Infinitive)
>We hope *to see the fair.* (Infinitive phrase)
>John said *that he cannot go.* (Noun clause)
>I know *who you are.* (Noun clause)

INDIRECT OBJECT

7. The *indirect object* names the person or thing that is
affected by the action of the verb on the object. It is
normally used with a verb that conveys such a meaning
as *give, offer, tell, allow, refuse, send, owe.* In the following examples the first italicized word is the indirect object and the second is the direct object:

>The florist gave *us* a dozen *roses.*
>The manager offered his *employees* a *share* in the profits.
>The dean refused *us permission* to leave early.
>You owe *me* five *dollars.*
>The instructor read the *class* a long *poem.*

8. The indirect object can generally be converted into
a prepositional phrase introduced by *to* and placed after
the direct object. Observe the following rewriting of two
of the sentences above:

>The florist gave a dozen roses *to us.*
>The instructor read a long poem *to the class.*

Such a phrase, however, is not called an indirect object. Only the object without preposition, standing between the verb and the direct object, is called an indirect object.

9. An indirect object is sometimes used without a direct object when the listener presumably can supply the missing object.

> I have told *him* (the news).
> Have you paid the *grocer* (the money)?

PREDICATE OBJECTIVE

10. The *predicate objective*, sometimes called the *objective complement*, is a second object that refers to the same person or thing named by the direct object. It is used in sentences with such verbs as *call, choose, make, name, think*. In the following examples the first italicized word is the direct object and the second is the predicate objective:

> The club chose *Mary president*.
> They named *Jane secretary*.
> You may make this *hotel* your *headquarters* for the convention.

11. The predicate objective usually shows the object as altered by the action of the verb, but there are some exceptions:

> We have always found *this* a satisfactory *hotel*.
> I consider *him* a very promising *novelist*.

12. You can generally identify a predicate objective by inserting *to be* between it and the object:

> The club chose Mary *to be* president.
> They named Jane *to be* secretary.

13. In some constructions a predicate objective may be introduced by *as:*

The club chose Mary *as president.*
The convention named the governor *as* temporary *chairman.*
We regard her *as* a competent *teacher.*

14. Nouns, pronouns, noun clauses, and gerunds or gerund phrases may be used as predicate objectives:

You may call this gadget a *doodler.*
What shall we call it?
You may call it *what you will.*
We call this sport *putting the shot.*

15. *Adjectives as Predicate Objectives.* Adjectives as well as nouns may be predicate objectives. These adjectives modify direct objects, but they always do so through the action expressed by the verbs. Usually they give the condition of the object brought about by the action of the verb.

We painted the roof *green.*
Our neighbors built the wall *high.*

But they do not always do so, as the following sentences show:

The rescuing party found the lost child *alive* and *unharmed.*
I consider him *courageous.*
Everyone regards him as *honest.* (*As* may introduce an adjective as well as a noun in this construction.)

16. A participle (verbal adjective) or an adjective phrase may serve as a predicate objective:

John kept us *guessing* about his plans.
We found the door *locked.*
A little work made the motor *of some use to us.*
We considered her new novel *of little value.*

17. NOTE: Observe carefully the difference between the following sentences:

> John held the lamp steady.
> John held the lamp steadily.

In the first, *steady* is an adjective used as predicate objective; it describes the lamp. In the second, *steadily* is an adverb modifying *held;* it describes John's manner of holding the lamp.

COGNATE OBJECT

18. A *cognate object* expresses a meaning similar to that expressed by the verb. It is used with verbs that do not otherwise take objects.

> She sighed a deep *sigh*.
> The children slept a peaceful *sleep*.
> I dreamed a *dream*.

RETAINED OBJECT

19. The object of a transitive verb in the passive voice is called a *retained object:*

> I was given this *pencil* by the instructor.

This object is said to be retained because it was the object of the verb in the active voice:

> The instructor gave me this *pencil*.

It is used only, as these examples indicate, with verbs that require in their active use both direct and indirect objects.

20. Either the direct or the indirect object may be retained:

> The instructor gave *me* this *pencil*. (The verb is in the active voice, with *pencil* as direct object and *me* as indirect.)

I was given this *pencil* by the instructor. (The direct object is retained, and the indirect object becomes the subject.)

This pencil was given *me* by the instructor. (The indirect object is retained, and the direct object becomes the subject.)

The clerk sold *me* the wrong book.

I was sold the wrong *book* by the clerk.

The wrong book was sold *me* by the clerk.

21. This construction with a retained object should be employed sparingly. Used frequently, it makes writing hard to read.

Predicate Noun

22. A *predicate noun* is a substantive used in the predicate to give another name — or the equivalent of a name — to the same person or thing named by the subject. In renaming the subject it restricts or explains the meaning expressed by the subject. The following sentence is an example:

Mr. Lane is a *doctor*.

Here the substantive *doctor* is another term to designate Mr. Lane, but it does more: it tells us something about Mr. Lane that the subject does not tell. The subject and predicate noun, in other words, refer to the same person — so much so that they might be interchanged, as in

A doctor is Mr. Lane.

Obviously, the predicate noun is not an object, since it neither receives nor results from the action expressed by the verb. It is used, in fact, only after a verb that indicates state or being instead of action.

23. The chief of these verbs is *be* in its several forms (*am, is, are, was, were*, etc.). This verb is often called a copulative verb, or copula, because it joins directly a word

in the predicate to the subject. Other words sometimes, but not always, used as copulative verbs are *become, seem, appear, prove, grow, look, sound*. (See Study Unit 5, paragraph 3.) These words are sometimes followed by a predicate noun, although more generally they are followed by a predicate adjective.

24. Though this type of complement is generally called a predicate noun, it may be any kind of substantive — that is, it may be a *noun, pronoun, gerund* or *gerund phrase, infinitive* or *infinitive phrase*, or *noun clause*. For this reason, it is sometimes referred to by the more inclusive name of *predicate substantive*. The various types are illustrated in the following sentences:

> Henry is *captain* of the team.
> I am *he* whom you called.
> His hopes proved *disappointments*.
> John seemed a *man*.
> My favorite sport is *fishing*.
> His greatest achievement was *building the Brooklyn bridge*.
> His only desire was *to leave*.
> Our problem is *to find a short route over the mountains*.
> Life is *what we make it*.
> My hope is *that we can leave tomorrow*.

25. CAUTION. Be careful not to use an adverbial clause erroneously as a predicate noun. Many people misuse *when*, *where*, and *because* clauses in this construction, as in the following sentences:

> Lobbying is when special groups exert pressure on Congress.
> Fratricide is where someone kills his brother.
> The reason I was absent yesterday is because my mother was ill.

Such sentences must be corrected either (1) by changing the adverbial construction to a substantive construction which can properly serve as a predicate noun or (2) by changing the first part of the sentence so that it can be properly modified by the adverbial clause. Thus the first sentence might become either of the two following sentences:

> Lobbying is the exertion of pressure on Congress by special groups.
>
> When special groups exert pressure on Congress they are said to lobby.

Sentences of the pattern "The reason . . . is because . . ." are especially frequent. The one above could be corrected in two ways:

> The reason I was absent yesterday is that my mother was ill. (Noun clause functions correctly as a predicate noun.)
>
> I was absent yesterday because my mother was ill. (Adverbial clause modifies *was absent* in the main clause.)

Predicate Adjective

26. A *predicate adjective* is an adjective used in the predicate to limit or describe the subject. It, too, occurs only with verbs that indicate state or being instead of action. A simple example is the following sentence:

> The boy is *good.*

The adjective *good* might be used before *boy*, as in *the good boy; good* describes the boy in one group as well as in the other. But *the good boy* is merely a label for the boy, whereas *The boy is good* is an assertion — a sentence. Other examples of predicate adjectives are as follows:

> The tree is *tall.*
> He will be *happy* when he gets the news.
> The horse became *lame.*
> The reasoning seems *correct.*
> Our hopes proved *futile.*
> The lights on the stage grew *bright.*
> The tire looked *old.*

27. When such words as *look*, *sound*, *feel*, *smell*, *stand*, and *taste* are used as copulas, you must be careful not to misuse an adverb after them in place of an adjective. An adverb may be used after these words only when it clearly describes the manner in which the action expressed by the verb takes place.

> Agnes looks beautiful in her new dress. (*Beautiful* states a quality or condition of the subject, just as if the sentence were *Agnes is beautiful in her new dress*.)
>
> He looked carefully at the paper. (Here *looked* is not a copula, and *carefully* describes the way in which the action of looking was performed.)
>
> The chimes sound clear. (This is equivalent to *The chimes are clear* or *The sound of the chimes is clear*.)
>
> I feel bad. (The meaning is similar to *I am in bad health* or *in a bad mood*. The adverb *badly* would indicate the manner of feeling; *I feel badly* would mean that the sense of touch is impaired.)
>
> I feel well. (Here *well* is an adjective, meaning *I am in good health*.)
>
> I feel good. (The statement means *I am in good spirits*.)
>
> The perfume smells bad. (*The perfume has a bad smell*.)
>
> The boy stands erect. (*The boy is erect*.)
>
> The boy stands firmly on the platform. (The sentence emphasizes the manner in which the boy performs the action of standing; hence the adverb *firmly* is used.)

EXERCISE 18. Identification of Complements

Point out each complement in the following sentences and tell what kind it is. (Some sentences have more than one complement, and some have none.)

1. The lightning struck the new house.
2. Mother made me a new dress.
3. We saw three good plays in New York.

4. The teacher said that we must read three of Stevenson's essays.
5. The French Club elected him secretary for the coming year.
6. My sister wrote me a ten-page letter.
7. All of the furniture in his office is new.
8. Clyde ran his third race in ten seconds.
9. They know where we live.
10. The committee transformed the ballroom into a mammoth igloo.
11. Esther bought ten yards of wide ribbon for her costume.
12. On our way to work we heard the band playing in the park.
13. My brother told me that you are going to the circus.
14. The bookcase is too tall for this room.
15. The play at the Broadway Theater this week is a depressing tragedy.
16. We went to the library immediately after the lecture.
17. John wants to go with us to the game.
18. Miss Perkins brought me a beautiful lace scarf from Holland.
19. Father always calls me Bill.
20. On our last trip to the farm we drove through deep mud.

EXERCISE 19.   Identification of Complements

Follow the instructions for Exercise 18.

On an automobile trip in the mountains last summer, we experienced an anxious half hour. Frankly, we were afraid. As we now look back upon the event, we know that we had only slight cause for our fear; but at the time we were not entirely rational. From these remarks you might conclude that we had a serious accident, and so I should say at once that nothing happened to us. We merely feared what might happen. I hope, however, that you will not misunderstand this statement. We were not victims of our imagination. The possibilities of danger were genuine. Literally, a single slip might have dashed us into eternity. Moreover, we were not hysterical or panicky. If we had been, you might call us cowards. The fact is that we were externally calm. There were five of us in the car, and yet no one revealed his uneasiness. This kind of conduct some people call "Spartan."

The cause of all our trouble was only the weather. The morning was warm and bright; but by noon a strong breeze was trying to sweep the clouds together. At that time we were beginning to ascend a long pass over the Continental Divide. The geography texts give it an authorized name; but we call it "Anxiety Pass." The road wound its way over the mountains by means of numerous horseshoe and hairpin turns. In places it was only a ledge cut in the rock. On the inside the wall went straight up; and on the outside, it went straight down. Along this outer edge there was no guard rail to keep cars from sliding off. Moreover, the road was being reconstructed. As yet the shoulders had not been made firm, and the surface had been only partly graveled. Since the roadbed had been graded, driving on it would have been simple in good weather; but the weather turned against us.

We should have known better than to go on. The clouds were becoming blacker, and the wind was beginning to blow ferociously; but we were so eager to get home before nightfall that we kept on going. Surely, a little rain ought not delay us. What we forgot, however, was that we had to climb four thousand feet to the top of the Pass. Well, several miles up the road, the rain began. Soon it was pouring; and the wind, rushing over the peaks and through the cañons, was swirling it about us. For a moment I thought that we were crossing the path of a tornado, even though I knew better. My experience reminded me that violent storms occur frequently in high altitudes; but this was the worst I had seen. Sitting in the back seat, I was able to make more observations than I could have made from my usual position at the wheel. All of us could see the water rushing down the road, and all could feel the swerving of the car on the slippery surface; but, looking at the road through the rear window, I alone saw patches of the outer edge crack off and fall into the cañon.

Though this edge seemed firm until we had passed, I wondered how long it would continue to be considerate of us. We would be safe enough, I knew, as long as we could drive in the middle of the road; but the question troubling me was what would happen if we met a car.

While I was thus pondering our prospects, the rain changed to hail. By this time we were undoubtedly three thousand feet higher, where the weather was colder. The white pellets bombarded our car and piled up against the windshield. They obscured the vision so much that the driver could scarcely see; but they were nothing compared to what followed. Soon the hail became snow. It was a heavy, wet snow that stuck wherever it lit. Consequently, the windshield was covered with so thick a layer that the wiper could scarcely make an opening. Because of the poor vision and the crumbling edge of the road, we should have stopped; but we feared that the car would slide backwards and drop off the road. While we were moving forward, we felt safer; and so we continued to go. Now I am glad that we did.

As is usual in these trying experiences, when our plight seemed to be at its worst, it was already becoming better. In a few minutes, the snow ceased falling; then we saw that we had reached the top. Now, on fairly level ground, stopping would be safe. As we pulled up beside the road, the sun began to shine feebly. This relief, after the long, silent strain, was a shock to our nervous system. We lost our self-control; and all of us simultaneously laughed a shrill, hysterical laugh. Ashamed of ourselves for the momentary lapse, we soon regained our composure and continued our trip without further hindrance.

☙ STUDY UNIT EIGHT

Modifying Elements

1. The three basic elements discussed in Study Units 5, 6, and 7 are equal in value. Though they are not independent of one another, their relationship is horizontal:

O----------O----------O

In both meaning and grammatical importance all other words in a sentence are subordinate to these three. (The only exceptions are independent elements and coordinate conjunctions connecting main clauses.) Their relationship to the basic elements may be said to be vertical; that is, they depend or "hang upon" the basic elements:

2. The most numerous class of these subordinate elements is *modifiers*.

Function of Modifiers

3. Every word in a sentence should convey as precisely as possible the exact meaning of the author; but often a single word, even with the most careful choice, does not in itself express the thought fully. To make its meaning more specific, it needs the assistance of other words, called *modifiers*. They sharpen the meanings of words. A *monument*, for example, may be more specifically referred to as a *shaft;* but the meaning of this word may be sharp-

ened by modifiers, such as *tall, slender, truncated, broken,* or *marble.* Likewise, the verb *to look* may be changed to the more specific verb *to stare,* the meaning of which may be sharpened by such modifiers as *blankly, weakly,* or *moodily.*

4. Modifiers are always either adjectives or adverbs. Adjectives modify nouns; adverbs modify verbs, adjectives, and other adverbs. Modifiers may be single words or groups of words.

Single Words as Modifiers

ADJECTIVES AND ADVERBS

5. The most familiar type of modifier is the single-word adjective or adverb, such as those italicized in the following sentences:

The *tri-motored* airplane droned *monotonously.*
The *four tall* boys sang *unusually well.*
He *suddenly* became *silent.*

6. The words illustrated above are regularly classified as adjectives or adverbs. In addition, words regularly classified as substantives may in special uses function as modifiers.

SUBSTANTIVE AS ADJECTIVE

7. Nouns are frequently used as adjectives simply by being placed before another noun.

Across the campus is the *chemistry* building. (*Chemistry* is normally classified as a noun, but its adjectival function here becomes clear if you expand it into "the building *for chemistry*" or "the building *for teaching chemistry.*")
She cleaned the kettle with *steel* wool.
We made a *picture* frame.
The *carpet* sweeper is broken.
John belongs to a *book* club.

Some such combinations appear so frequently that they come to be thought of as a unit, and sometimes to be written as a single word: *airplane, textbook, newspaper, birdhouse, bloodhound.*

8. The possessive form of a noun is used as an adjective, modifying the thing possessed:

> A *boy's* ambitions are sometimes fantastic.
> The *girls'* voices were coarse.
> *George's* new hat is too small.

SUBSTANTIVE AS ADVERB

9. A noun may also be used as an adverb, modifying a verb, an adjective, or another adverb, in certain constructions indicating limitation or extent of time, space, measure, weight, or degree.

> Fred must travel many *weeks* before he returns.   (Modifies the verb *travel.*)
> Some New England villages are three *centuries* older than our town.   (Modifies the adjective *older.*)
> Since noon the water has risen seven *inches.*   (Modifies the verb *has risen.*)
> They arrived a *week* late.   (Modifies the adverb *late.*)
> The pole must be ten *feet* long.   (Modifies the adjective *long.*)

10. NOTE: Other substantives besides nouns, of one word or more, may likewise be used adverbially.

> We went *swimming.*   (Gerund modifies the verb *went.*)
> He is sure *to come.*   (Infinitive modifies the adjective *sure.*)
> The chairman is certain *to table the motion.*   (Infinitive phrase modifies the adjective *certain.*)
> We rejoiced *that you had won the game.*   (Noun clause modifies the verb *rejoiced.*)
> We are glad *that you are here.*   (Noun clause modifies the adjective *glad.*)

Groups of Words as Modifiers

11. Groups of words, as well as single words, are regularly used as adjective and adverbial modifiers. When a group is a modifier, it functions as a unit. Each group serves exactly as would a single-word adjective or adverb.

12. There are two groups used as modifiers: *phrases* and *subordinate clauses.*

PHRASES

13. *Prepositional*, *participial*, and *infinitive phrases* may serve as adjective modifiers. In the following sentences the italicized phrases modify the nouns preceding them:

> The building *on the hill* is the library. (Prepositional phrase)
>
> The man *with the transit* is the foreman. (Prepositional phrase)
>
> We saw John *driving his new car.* (Participial phrase)
>
> The work *begun last week* was finished today. (Participial phrase)
>
> The person *to see this report* is the superintendent. (Infinitive phrase)
>
> The houses *to be sold in October* are small and comfortable. (Infinitive phrase)

14. *Prepositional* and *infinitive phrases* may be used as adverbial modifiers. In each of the following sentences the italicized phrase modifies a verb:

> Every machine functioned *with human skill.* (Prepositional phrase)
>
> Our train went *through a long tunnel.* (Prepositional phrase)
>
> We drove a long way *to see the mountains.* (Infinitive phrase)
>
> We pushed the car *to start the motor.* (Infinitive phrase)

15. *Subordinate clauses* may be used as either adjective or adverbial modifiers.

> Miners *who work all day* seldom see the sun. (Adjective modifying the noun *miners*)
> The instructor assigned the lesson *that we had studied.* (Adjective modifying the noun *lesson*)
> Our car skidded *because the pavement was wet.* (Adverb modifying the verb *skidded*)
> *When the orchestra has played the next number*, I shall go home. (Adverb modifying the verb *shall go*)

Number and Variety of Modifiers

16. A word may have as many modifiers as it needs to sharpen its meaning sufficiently, and these modifiers may be of one type or several.

> The low, rambling house on the edge of town deteriorated rapidly because it was shamefully neglected.
> That tall young man who is standing in front of the window has just returned to college after several years in the army.

Here single words, phrases, and clauses modify the basic elements.

Relationship to Basic Elements

17. All modifiers in a sentence are related to one or another of the basic elements, either directly or indirectly.

DIRECT MODIFIERS

18. The simplest relationship is direct, in which the modifier is attached immediately to the basic element. In the first example in paragraph 16, the relationship of

the modifiers to the basic elements may be analyzed as
follows:

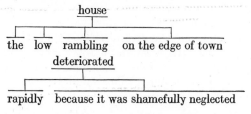

Here the two modifiers that are not single words, *on the
edge of town* and *because it was shamefully neglected*, are
considered as units, the first modifying *house* as a single adjective would, the second modifying *deteriorated* as a single
adverb would.

INDIRECT MODIFIERS

19. But the relationship of the words in this sentence
may be more fully analyzed as follows:

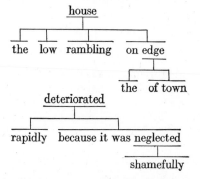

You observe that in a prepositional phrase which modifies a basic element, the object of the preposition may itself have modifiers, and that similarly in a clause which is
a modifier the basic elements may in turn have modifiers.

20. In other words, some modifiers are related to the
basic elements of a sentence indirectly by being attached

immediately to direct modifiers; such indirect modifiers may in their turn have modifiers, and so on. An indirect modifier may thus be removed from a direct modifier of a basic element by several intervening modifiers. But however far removed, its function is ultimately to amplify or restrict the meaning of the direct modifier and, through it, to modify a basic element.

21. This relationship is illustrated by an analysis of the following sentence:

> The gaily dressed band from Rarden, which is a little town at the northern end of Lake Dunstan, easily won first award in the annual contest that the University conducts for the small schools of the state.

The basic elements of this sentence are as follows:

> *Subject:* band
> *Verb:* won
> *Complement (Object):* award

All other words are added to make more specific the meaning of this simple sentence: *Band won award.* These words, excepting connectives, are either direct or indirect modifiers, related to one another and to the basic elements as shown in the following analysis:

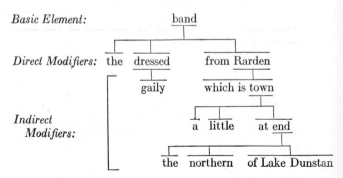

Basic Element: band

Direct Modifiers: the   dressed   from Rarden
                              gaily   which is town

Indirect Modifiers: a   little   at end
                                    the   northern   of Lake Dunstan

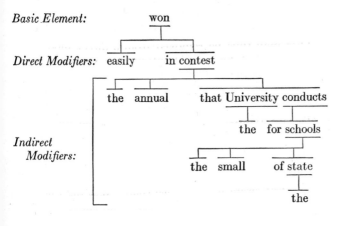

Basic Element: won

Direct Modifiers: easily   in contest

Indirect Modifiers: the   annual   that University conducts   the   for schools   the   small   of state   the

Basic Element: award

Direct Modifier: first

Exercise 20. Modifiers of Basic Elements

Point out the basic elements in each of the following sentences; then show how the modifying elements are related to them.

1. A team of horses slowly pulled the car into town.
2. Three small, dirty windows in one wall of the room grudgingly provided a dim, gray light.
3. A crowd of people were eagerly watching the bulletin board in the window of the newspaper office for reports on the flood.
4. The book on art that I bought when I was in Paris explains clearly the beginnings of impressionistic painting.
5. In the high altitudes of the Continental Divide, when the wind blows fiercely, twisted pine trees hug the rocky slopes of the mountains as if they were groping for support.

6. An artist painting a picture must always see clearly the image that he wants to put on his canvas.
7. Sitting upon a rock, a sleek, fat chipmunk was calmly gnawing the shell of an almond.
8. When they entered the room, the excited children saw a beautifully decorated Christmas tree with numerous packages piled around it.
9. All of the guests at the recital applauded his playing of the sonata because it expressed deep feeling.
10. John Keats, who struggled vainly against a devastating disease, achieved a lasting reputation in his few years of life because he wrote some of the most beautiful poetry in the English language.

EXERCISE 21.   Modifiers of Basic Elements

Follow the instructions for Exercise 20.

The largest crowd of the season was waiting tensely for the opening of the championship football game. Nearly every student, hundreds of townspeople, and visitors from all parts of the state were there. Most eager and most demonstrative, of course, were the students. In the center section of the grandstand they were seated in a prearranged order. On the front seats, a group of about fifty young men in red and white striped coats formed the nucleus. Apparently they were chosen for their special ability to make noise. Behind this group were sitting other young men without uniforms. Many of them, however, wore gaily colored sweaters and caps. They, no doubt, were the assistants to those in uniform. At any rate, they gave that impression. They always did what those in the other group did. On either side of these groups was a section or two of girls. Down upon the ground in front of the men's section were three young men who were dressed alike in light-blue flannel coats and white trousers. Each was holding a large megaphone. The young man in the center, who seemed to be the leader, raised his megaphone to his mouth. Few people except those in front of him heard what he said. Apparently, though, he was giving instructions. Throwing his megaphone upon the ground, he stretched his arms high above his head. Simultaneously the entire group of students rose and yelled lustily. All three young men had now thrown aside their megaphones, and, with their arms upstretched, they were weaving their bodies rhythmically from side to side. Suddenly they stood still, and the students promptly stopped their noise and sat down. Within a few seconds, however, a high, tense voice shrieked something that was unintelligible; but it must have been a signal for action. Immediately everyone stood and shouted independently; the band played the varsity march, and the three young men with the megaphones danced and jumped and turned somersaults. Everyone, of course, knows what was happening. The home team was trotting down the center of the field.

❧ STUDY UNIT NINE

Connective Elements

1. Connective elements are coupling pins in a sentence. Consisting of words or groups of words, they join words, phrases, and clauses, and show the relationship between the parts that they connect. Hence they are not merely little insignificant words in a sentence, but necessary elements.

2. There are three classes of connective elements: *prepositions*, *coordinate conjunctions*, and *subordinate connectives*.

Prepositions

3. As you already know, a preposition joins a substantive, called its object, to another word in the sentence and shows how it is related to this other word. Many prepositions indicate spatial or temporal relationships; the other types of relationship which they express can be observed in the following list of the most commonly used prepositions:

ONE-WORD PREPOSITIONS

about	before	by
above	behind	concerning
across	below	despite
after	beneath	down
against	beside, besides	during
along	between	except, excepting
around	beyond	for
at	but (meaning "except")	from

in
inside
into
notwithstanding
of
off
on
outside

over
past
round
since
through
throughout
to, into
toward, towards

under
underneath
until, till
up
upon
with
within
without

COMPOUND PREPOSITIONS

according to
along with
apart from
as for, as to
aside from
because of
by means of
by reason of
by way of
for the sake of
from above
from among

from between
from under
in accordance with
in addition to
in case of
in compliance with
in consideration of
in front of
in opposition to
in place of
in preference to
in regard to

in spite of
inside of
instead of
on account of
out from
out of
outside of
over against
up to
with reference to
with regard to
with respect to

4. The preceding Study Unit has shown that prepositional phrases may serve either as adjectives or as adverbs. In an adjective phrase the preposition connects its object with a noun; in an adverbial phrase, with a verb, an adjective, or another adverb.

> The book *on the table* is mine. (Adjective, modifying the noun *book*)
> The horse jumped *over the fence*. (Adverb, modifying the verb *jumped*)
> He was eager *for reward*. (Adverb, modifying the adjective *eager*)
> It is too late *for the trip*. (Adverb, modifying the adverb *too*)

5. NOTE: You will observe that in a prepositional phrase a connective element is really a part of a modifying element. The modifier is a complete phrase, one of the elements of which is a connective. We will find the same overlapping between modifiers and connectives when we come to subordinate clauses that function as modifiers.

Coordinate Conjunctions

6. Coordinate conjunctions (*and, but, or, nor*, and the correlatives *either . . . or, neither . . . nor, not only . . . but also, both . . . and*) join words, phrases, or clauses of equal (coordinate) rank.

> The president *and* the secretary had seats on the platform. (Joins coordinate subjects.)
>
> The ball is made of yarn *and* rubber. (Joins coordinate objects of the preposition *of*.)
>
> Standing upon the edge of the swimming pool, he lost his balance *and* splashed into the water. (Joins coordinate parts of the predicate.)
>
> The chimney sweep has soot on his face *and* in his hair. (Joins coordinate phrases.)
>
> In preparing for the picnic they agreed that the girls would buy the wieners *and* that the boys would roast them. (Joins dependent clauses of equal value.)
>
> The boys went early to build a fire for the wiener roast, *and* the girls followed an hour later. (Joins two coordinate main clauses.)
>
> Some of the boys wanted to leave at five o'clock, *but* most of them could not go until six. (From the point of view of the thought, *but* does not join parts of a sentence. Because it shows contrast, it separates them. Grammatically, however, it joins. In this example it connects two coordinate main clauses.)
>
> Do you want gloves *or* shoes for Christmas? (*Or* and *nor*, like *but*, show contrast or alternate conditions, but grammatically they connect parts of a sentence. Here the *or* connects coordinate objects of *do want*.)

I want *either* gloves *or* shoes.   (*Either* and *or* are correlatives joining the coordinate objects of *want*.)

I want *neither* gloves *nor* shoes.   (*Neither* and *nor* are also correlatives joining the coordinate objects of *want*, but they express a negative thought.   Note that the correlative of *neither* is always *nor*.)

Subordinate Connectives

7. Subordinate connectives join dependent clauses to main clauses.

8. A dependent clause, you remember, is always a part of speech in a sentence, used as a noun, an adjective, or an adverb.   That is, it may serve either as a substantive or as a modifier in a sentence.   In a study of connectives it is useful to consider these two groups separately.

WORDS INTRODUCING NOUN CLAUSES

9. Actually, when a subordinate clause serves as a substantive (that is, as subject, appositive, predicate noun, or object of a verb or preposition), the word that introduces it cannot be said in any significant sense to connect it with another part of the sentence.   When it is used as the object of a preposition, the preposition connects it with the main clause.   When it is used as a basic element or as an appositive, it does not need a connective any more than if it were a one-word substantive.

10. For example, the subordinate conjunction *that* at the beginning of such a clause simply introduces the clause and gives notice that it is a subordinate clause.

> *That you won the race* is certain.   (The clause serves as subject.)
> The truth is *that you won the race*.   (Predicate noun)
> We know *that you won the race*.   (Object of verb)

Noun clauses may also be introduced by other types of words which, unlike *that*, serve within their clauses as parts of speech, either as substantives or as adverbs.

11. *Noun Clauses Introduced by Pronouns.* From your study of pronouns, you are already familiar with noun clauses introduced by relative and interrogative pronouns. Observe in the following sentences that these pronouns do not serve as connectives but instead function as substantives within the dependent clauses.

> I wonder *who did this.* (The interrogative pronoun *who* is the subject of the noun clause, which in turn is the direct object in the main clause.)
>
> I wonder *who he is.* (Here *who* is the predicate pronoun.)
>
> *What you say* is true. (Since the relative pronoun *what* is equivalent to *that which*, the clause is equivalent to a substantive plus a modifying clause: *that which you say.* But strictly speaking, *what you say* is a noun clause serving as subject of the sentence, and *what* functions in the noun clause as direct object.)

12. *Noun Clauses Introduced by Adverbs.* Noun clauses may also be introduced by *when, where, why, how, whence, whither,* which do not perform a true connective function but instead serve as adverbs within their clauses. Consider, for example, the following sentence:

> The foreman told me where I could find some tools.

The idea of place contained in *where* does not affect the logical relationship of the subordinate clause to the main clause; instead, it is related to the verb of the subordinate clause. (The situation is different where these words introduce modifying clauses, as you will see later.) Other examples are the following:

> *How* the votes are counted is a mystery to everyone.
> His first question was *when* we should leave for the show.
> *Why* you should think so is inexplicable.

WORDS INTRODUCING MODIFYING CLAUSES

13. When a subordinate clause serves as an adjective or an adverb, it modifies a single word (or group of words)

just as if it were a single-word adjective or adverb. The word that introduces the clause connects the clause with the word which it modifies and reveals its relationship to that word. Such connectives fall into two groups: subordinate conjunctions and relative pronouns.

14. *Clauses Introduced by Subordinate Conjunctions.* An adverbial clause is regularly introduced by a subordinate conjunction that joins it to the word which it modifies and shows how its thought is related to that word by indicating whether it expresses cause, purpose, condition, etc. The following are the most commonly used subordinate conjunctions:

ONE-WORD SUBORDINATE CONJUNCTIONS

after	since	when
although	than	whenever
as	that	where
because	though	whereas
before	till	wherever
if	unless	while
lest	until	

COMPOUND SUBORDINATE CONJUNCTIONS

as if	even if	provided that
as though	in case that	so that
but that	in order that	

15. Some examples of their use follow:

CAUSE: The pen leaked because it was cracked.
PURPOSE: We stayed at home so that we could study.
CONDITION: The clock will run if you wind it.
MANNER: The horse limped as if he were lame.
TEMPORAL RELATIONSHIP: He came after the guests had left.
CONCESSION: Though he has many good qualities, I have never liked him.

16. *Clauses Introduced by Relative Pronouns.* Most adjective clauses are introduced by relative pronouns, which serve simultaneously as connectives, as pronouns standing in place of their antecedents, and as substantives in their own clauses. Consider the following sentence:

The man *who was here yesterday* is my uncle.

Who serves three functions in the sentence. (1) As a pronoun, it stands for *man*, its antecedent, and makes unnecessary the repetition of that noun. (2) As a connective, it introduces a relative clause which serves as an adjective modifier of the antecedent and it joins the clause to this substantive. (3) As a substantive, it serves as the subject of the relative clause. The following sentences illustrate various functions of the relative in its clause:

The people *who arrived late* could not find seats. (Subject)
The people *whom you met* arrived late. (Direct object)
The people *to whom you gave your seats* were grateful. (Object of preposition)

17. NOTE: Adjective clauses are sometimes introduced by *where, when, why* in sentences of the following pattern:

This is the house *where* I was born.
Tomorrow is the day *when* the examinations begin.
The reason *why* the library is closed is that our vacation began today.

Such clauses are really telescoped relative clauses, since *where, when, why* are equivalent in these cases to *in which, on which, for which.* In such sentences *where, when, why* serve both as connectives and as parts of speech (in this case, as adverbs) within their clauses.

Classification Determined by Use

18. You have doubtless observed by this time that it is often impossible to classify a connective by its form, since some words are used in two or more different ways. For example, some words may be used both as prepositions and as adverbs.

> The boys have just come *in*.   (Adverb)
> They are *in* the house now.   (Preposition)

Some words may be used both as prepositions and as conjunctions.

> They arrived *after* me.
> They arrived *after* I did.

Some words may introduce both independent and dependent clauses.

> *Who* are you?
> I want to know *who* you are.

Subordinate connectives may serve different functions.

> He asked when I could come.   (Here *when* introduces a noun clause, within which it serves as an adverb modifying *could come*.)
> He came when I least expected him.   (Here *when* introduces an adverbial clause, which it connects with the main clause, and expresses the temporal relation between the two clauses.)
> This is the day when the assignment is due.   (Here *when* introduces an adjective clause, which it connects with *day* and within which it serves as an adverb.)

Hence it is essential that you analyze the use of the word within its sentence before you attempt to classify it.

Exercise 22.   Connective Elements

Identify each connective in the following sentences by stating whether it is a preposition, a coordinate conjunction, or a subordinate connective.

1. Six students made the scenery and costumes for the play that the Thespian Club gave last week.
2. Paper and ink were furnished for the quiz, but students were expected to bring their own pens.
3. When we drove to Chicago last week, we found miles of the paved road covered with sleet.
4. A jeweler who sells precious stones can shrewdly estimate the current value of any diamond that he sees.
5. The men whom we met in the shelter house had climbed to the top of the mountain before breakfast.
6. In this issue of the alumni magazine we ought to print a picture of the men's or the women's dormitory.
7. We were glad that we went to the matinee because the leading lady became ill suddenly before the evening performance.
8. Since my brother lost the key to the ignition switch, we do not know how to start the car.
9. The instructor wanted to know why I had not submitted my paper when it was due.
10. Many of the old books in the library ought to be rebound, but a few of them are not worth keeping.
11. Thomas Hardy, novelist and poet, was eighty-eight years of age when he died.
12. When we sat down at our desks, we found that someone had put a pen, a bottle of ink, and a blotter on each one; but we could not use the pens because they had old-fashioned steel points that scratched.
13. Our directions were that we should get off the bus at the entrance to the campus, follow the main walk to Woodbine Hall — the name of which was on a brass plate beside the door — and then take a cinder path that went diagonally across the quadrangle to the Fisher Memorial Aquarium.
14. The members of the committee who were given the task of arranging a picnic for the senior class in either April or May chose May 2, which came on Saturday; but when the day arrived it was so cold and wet that no one wanted to go.

15. *The Log of a Cowboy* by Andy Adams, who rode the open range long before he became a writer, is a fascinating record of one phase of western life in the 1880's because it deals simply and accurately — but also creatively — with the experiences of cowboys in driving several thousand cattle from Texas to Montana.

16. Along the ridge of the Green Mountains in Vermont, which extend north and south through the entire length of the state, is a trail for hikers.

17. When classes were resumed on Monday morning after the spring vacation, a steam shovel in the next block was making so much noise that no one could hear the instructor.

18. Richard Steele, an English journalist, essayist, and playwright who was born in 1672, has a distinguished reputation of his own; but his name is generally associated with that of Joseph Addison because both of them founded the *Spectator*, a publication for which they wrote some interesting and entertaining essays.

19. On the western bank of Lake Champlain, which at this point is the boundary between New York and Vermont, stands Fort Ticonderoga, the scene of many important battles in the French and Indian War, but now a museum for relics of colonial days.

20. Preeminent in American letters as lecturer, writer, and philosopher is Ralph Waldo Emerson, who lived in Concord, Massachusetts, where he and his friends Thoreau and Alcott became the nucleus of a group that has been known as the Concord School of Philosophy or as the Transcendentalist Group.

EXERCISE 23.   Connective Elements

Follow the instructions for Exercise 22.

While I was touring in the East, I had one of those embarrassing moments that come to all of us occasionally. I might have been nonchalant about it, but it came so suddenly that

I was bewildered. My partner and I had been driving all day, and we were tired. We should have been at the end of our journey, but we had been delayed by a long detour, which was over rough macadam roads. The result was that in the late afternoon, when cars were swarming in the streets, we had to drive through a crowded city. It was not large, but it was in a densely populated area, all of which was strange to us. Since we were not familiar with the route, we went wherever the map directed us to go.

As we entered the outskirts of the city, we found ourselves on a wide six-lane boulevard. By chance we got into the middle lane going south. We preferred the outer lane; but, since every lane was crowded, with cars almost bumper to bumper, we stayed where we happened to be. We probably could have got out of our lane if we had tried, but we did not want to cause any confusion; nor did we want to intensify the obviously ruffled tempers of the drivers, most of whom honked their horns impatiently at every slight delay, especially when the car at the head of a line did not move promptly after a traffic light had changed to green. In spite of this noise I was unruffled. Compared with the detour, the paving was as smooth as a ballroom floor; and the car seemed to roll forward without power. I knew that by merely going along with the other cars, which were moving at a good speed, we should soon be out of the city.

When we came to the next traffic signal, however, the "moment" that I referred to had arrived. As the green light changed to yellow, the car ahead of me sped across a wide intersecting boulevard, leaving me at the head of the line. Automatically I pushed down on the brake and clutch pedals. The car stopped properly; but suddenly I had a sinking, helpless feeling. The clutch pedal had gone down to the floor, and there it stayed. When the red light changed to green, moreover, there the car stayed, at the head of the middle lane on a crowded boulevard, with a thousand cars behind — so I thought — honking their imprecations.

Appositive Elements

1. An appositive is a substantive that is associated with another substantive and refers to the same person or thing to which the first substantive refers. Its purpose is to amplify, limit, or explain the first. The second word is said to be in apposition with the first.

> My eldest brother, *John*, is visiting in Cincinnati. (*John* is in apposition with *brother*.)

2. An appositive usually follows the substantive with which it is in apposition, but it may precede it.

> A *man* highly respected in his community, my uncle was elected at one time or another to every important office. (*Man* is in apposition with *uncle*.)

3. An appositive may be used wherever a substantive is used, as subject, predicate noun, object of verb, or object of preposition.

4. Because of its function in a sentence an appositive has a double nature. It functions somewhat as a modifier of the substantive with which it is in apposition, for it expands or limits its meaning much as a modifier would. This is made clear when we convert an appositive into a dependent adjective clause of equivalent meaning:

> My eldest brother, John, is visiting in Cincinnati.
> My eldest brother, whose name is John, is visiting in Cincinnati.

St. Paul, the capital of Minnesota, is on the Mississippi River.

St. Paul, which is the capital of Minnesota, is on the Mississippi River.

On the other hand, since the appositive gives a substitute name for the substantive with which it is in apposition, it is to be thought of, not as subordinate (as a modifier would be), but as equal to that word. If it is in apposition with the subject of a sentence, it is equivalent to a subject, and so on. It is always in the same case as the word with which it is in apposition.

Kinds of Appositives

5. Any kind of substantive may be an appositive. The following sentences illustrate various kinds:

That tree in our front yard, an *oak*, was planted by my grandfather. (Noun)

One healthful exercise for young men, *running*, is too strenuous for old people. (Gerund)

His first impulse, *to leave*, was ignoble. (Infinitive)

The president's announcement *that the Christmas holiday would be cut short* was greeted with groans. (Clause)

Appositive Phrases

6. An appositive, like other substantives, frequently has words related to it. Nouns and pronouns used as appositives may have any type of adjective modifier. Verbals used as appositives — gerunds and infinitives — may have adverbial modifiers as well, and may also have complements. The simple appositive and all the words related to it form an *appositive phrase*.

Those old seafaring people, *the rugged Vikings from Scandinavia whose life was lived at sea*, were intrepid explorers. (Noun with adjective modifiers as appositive)

The doctor at the hospital, *the old one with the gray beard*, is a distinguished surgeon.   (Pronoun with adjective modifiers as appositive)

John's favorite hobby, *flying a large airplane across country*, is expensive.   (Gerund phrase as appositive)

His final decision, *to leave the meeting suddenly without a word*, took everyone by surprise.   (Infinitive phrase as appositive)

Appositives with Introductory Words

7. Now and then an appositive is preceded by words that introduce it, such as *or*, *as*, *namely*, *that is*, and *for example*.   These introductory words are considered a part of the appositive phrase.

A thermostat, *or mechanism for controlling temperature*, opens and closes the shutters.

We demand that you, *as president*, call a meeting of the society.

I have two favorite hobbies, *namely*, *gardening and stamp collecting*.

Only one person in the class, *that is*, *John Smith*, has finished his paper.

The doctor told us to eat a variety of fresh vegetables — *for example*, *carrots, spinach, and lettuce*.

Much of the clothing that we took on our fishing trip, *such as heavy sweaters and raincoats*, we did not need.

Notice that *namely* and *that is* can be omitted from such sentences without changing the sense, but that *for example* and *such as* cannot.   The appositive following *for example* or *such as* is said to be partial or incomplete.

Types of Substantives That May Have Appositives

8. An appositive may be in apposition with any kind of substantive, as illustrated by the italicized substantives in the following sentences:

We drove to *Peterborough*, a town in New Hampshire. (Noun)

The convention chose *all* who had been nominated, two women and three men. (Pronoun)

Rowing, my favorite sport, is very invigorating. (Gerund)

Reading two chapters, the usual daily assignment, required two hours. (Gerund phrase)

To leave — a tempting possibility — would have been a serious mistake. (Infinitive)

To be hungry, a hardship I have never experienced, was his daily lot. (Infinitive phrase)

The dean announced *that the holidays would be extended*, a statement that was greeted with cheers. (Clause)

9. A peculiar kind of appositional relationship is that in which a noun clause, coming generally at the end of a sentence, is in apposition with an expletive *it*.

It is commonly known that oil will float upon water.

It is true that we walked from Kansas City to St. Louis

EXERCISE 24. Appositives and Appositive Phrases

In the following sentences identify each appositive and the substantive with which it is in apposition. If the appositive is a phrase, show how the elements in it are related.

1. The picture on the east wall, a rare old lithograph, was given me by my grandfather.

2. The old mountain railroad between Goldland and Silver Gulch, that is, the Denver, Rockfield and Western, was dismantled in 1920.

3. We have decided on our next move — to leave this town as soon as we can pack our clothes.

4. Suddenly we heard a deafening confusion of sound, a sharp jangling of many bells.

5. A well-known axiom of geometry — that a straight line is the shortest distance between two points — is a good guide for writers.

6. Directly under the ceiling in my room are three small windows, mere holes in the wall, placed so high that no one can look out.

7. Coming from the newspaper office opposite our hotel, the rhythmical clatter of the automatic presses, a regular beating of metal upon metal, continued so far into the night that we could not sleep.

8. All of the children at the Christmas party — the entire sixth grade of the Whittier School — received a present.

9. Our new dictionary, a large volume of more than three thousand pages, is a gift from Aunt Alice.

10. Everybody in the audience — men, women, and children — joined the chorus in singing Christmas carols.

11. The walls and the ceiling of the auditorium were covered with a new kind of plaster, a fibrous material designed to prevent echoes.

12. The chief thought of his essay, that editorials in our newspapers have less influence upon the reading public than did those of fifty years ago, is well developed.

13. Slowly and cautiously we descended the steep mountainside, dragging a huge log, the trunk of a tree that the wind had blown over.

14. He cut himself as he was shaving with his new razor, a kind that is supposed to be safe.

15. Her brother John, whom you met last summer, has gone to Australia.

16. The MacDowell Colony, a haven for artists and writers who want a quiet place to work undisturbed, is in New Hampshire.

17. It is assumed that Shakespeare was born on April 23, 1564.

18. The coach gave him his instructions for the last lap — to sprint as much as he could.

19. This book, *Adam Bede*, which is a novel by George Eliot, is an illustrated edition.

20. He wrote a letter on foolscap paper, an extra long shee
used generally for legal documents.

21. The carburetor, or device for vaporizing gasoline, is some
times called the heart of an automobile.

22. We soon saw what had happened by glancing hastily
through the article in the newspaper, a task that require
only a few minutes.

23. Tom sold ten tickets to the masked ball, the most colorfu
dance of the season.

24. We mixed the three primary colors, namely, red, yellow
and blue.

25. A highly exaggerated character who is always expectin
better fortune, Micawber reminds us of people we know

Exercise 25. Appositives and Appositive Phrases

Follow the instructions for Exercise 24.

On a recent automobile trip over the Rocky Mountains w
found ourselves in an unexpected situation, one that we me
in an unusual manner. Leaving home about ten o'clock i
the morning of a bright, crisp September day, we planned t
drive to a mountain resort so that we could stay all night in
small cabin, which we had already engaged. Knowing tha
most of the bedding would be furnished, we had taken wit
us only a couple of blankets apiece. If we had even faintl
suspected that we might have to sleep outside, we should hav
taken more, because we knew from experience how cold
September night can be at an altitude of nine thousand feet —
an elevation of nearly two miles above sea level. That ex
perience was what caused us to reserve the cabin. The roads
however, were rougher than we had expected; and darknes
overtook us by the time that we arrived at the first town o
the western side of the Divide, a small straggly settlemen
fifteen or twenty miles from our destination. Being too tire
to drive over rough mountain roads in the dark, we decide

to try in this little town to rent a cabin in which we could sleep for the night and cook our supper and breakfast.

As we came into the town, consisting of only a couple dozen widely separated houses and a few stores, we thought that we saw some vacant cabins, and so we inquired about them at the stores, the only public places to which we could go for information. At the last of these stores we found the owner, a grizzled old man smoking a corncob pipe, who told us that all of the cabins had been engaged for the night. Then we first had visions of ourselves lying under the stars with only a couple of blankets over us — a pair of thin blankets. After a few more inquiries, however, we were able to rent, not a cabin, but a house — a five-room, two-story frame building that was set apart from the other houses at the edge of town. This house, we were told, was completely furnished. As you might expect, our spirits began to rise at once.

When we saw it, though, we were disappointed, because it was so untidy and musty that we never could have slept or eaten in it. What we were to do, we did not know. We were certain, of course, that we did not want to travel any farther; and we were equally certain that we did not want to sleep on the cold ground. At length, someone in the group — my brother, I think — suggested that we could escape the odor of the house and still keep ourselves off the ground by taking the mattresses, which were clean, into the back yard and sleeping there. No other house being close to ours, all of us thought that the proposal was a good one; and so we dragged the mattresses outside, laid them beside the car, and made our bed for the night. Then we built a fire and cooked our supper, a simple meal, consisting chiefly of bacon and eggs. As soon as we had finished and had packed the utensils in the car, we lay down under the stars to sleep.

Being tired, we went to sleep promptly; but after a short time, probably no more than half an hour, we were wakened by riotous noises, such as the barking of dogs, the bellowing of cows, and the irregular clanking of cow bells. All of us sat up, startled by the bedlam. In our half-sleep we thought that the whole world had gone mad; but we soon discovered that some dogs were chasing cows in a circle about our house. Not one of us fellows, however, had sense enough to do anything until my brother John, who seemed to be more widely awake than the rest of us, threw some rocks at the dogs and drove them away. Quiet and peace were restored; but when we lay down again, sleep was gone. The full moon, a large white porcelain plate with queer figures on it, was reflecting the bright light in our faces; and the cold air was penetrating our thin blankets. Some of us, my brother and I, tried to sleep; but the others built up the fire and sat around it until dawn.

Those who never have gone through an uncomfortable night cannot know how relieved we were when we saw the first glimmer of day, the faint gray light in the East, scarcely able to compete with the crisp white light of the moon, which had not yet disappeared. We were so eager to be on our way that we, though still tired and sleepy, quietly put the blankets into the car, returned the mattresses to their beds in the house, and left for the place where we should have been.

Independent Elements

1. An independent element is so named because it has no grammatical relationship to any specific word in the sentence. Nevertheless, it must often be inserted in a sentence to restrict, amplify, or clarify the meaning of the sentence or to show its relationship to another sentence. It sometimes serves as a modifier of the entire sentence. Most of the specific functions of the independent element are included in the following list:

2. *To state names or titles used in direct address:*

> *Fred,* I need my pencil.
> *Mr. Chairman,* I move that the motion be tabled.
> I move, *ladies and gentlemen,* that the motion be adopted.
> I am positive, *John,* that the show begins at eight o'clock.

3. *To express feeling by means of interjections or other exclamations that clearly belong with the thought of the sentence:*

> *Ah,* now I have the answer.
> *Hush!* Mother is asleep.
> All of my examinations, *worse luck,* come at the end of the week.
> *Hurrah!* You have won the prize.

4. *To attract attention or to summarize the thought of a sentence by means of an introductory word:*

> *Well,* let's go.
> *Here,* you take this seat.
> *Why,* I think I'll be able to go.

> *Yes*, I agree with you.
> *No*, we did not win the game.

5. *To provide a transition, by means of an adverb between a sentence and the one preceding it in a paragraph.* Because this adverb shows the relationship between the thoughts of the two sentences, it is often called a conjunctive adverb.

> We now know, *however*, that the theory was wrong.
> We must go, *then*, as soon as the car arrives.
> The answer, *therefore*, is correct.
> He has, *moreover*, prepared his assignment for tomorrow.
> I shall, *nevertheless*, refuse to go.

6. *To comment upon, qualify, contradict, interrupt, or emphasize the thought of a sentence by injecting a word, a phrase, or another sentence.* This injected expression, sometimes called a parenthetical element, is clearly related to the thought of the sentence in which it appears, often serving as a modifier of the entire thought; but it is grammatically unrelated to the sentence.

> *Unfortunately*, we were unable to get reserved seats.
> Our decision, *of course*, may be wrong.
> We had, *unluckily*, forgotten the spare tire.
> Your explanation is, *indeed*, clear.
> His acting, *to be sure*, is better than it was five years ago.
> He told my brother — *I heard him myself* — that he was going to New York.
> The new school song (*have you heard it yet?*) is full of life.
> The song, *you know*, was written by Fred.
> This song, *I tell you*, is full of life.
> A participial phrase — *I assume that you know what one is* — must modify a substantive.

7. CAUTION. Be careful not to confuse these injected expressions with appositives and with dependent clauses.

> His new car — *it has red wheels* — is sturdy. (The italicized words form an independent element, a grammati-

cally complete sentence inserted into another complete sentence.)

His new car, *the one with the red wheels*, is sturdy. (The italicized words form an appositive phrase in apposition with *car*.)

His new car, *which has red wheels*, is sturdy. (The italicized words form a dependent relative clause grammatically connected with *car* as an adjective modifier.)

8. Remember that any part of a sentence grammatically related to a word in the sentence is not an independent element, even though it contains an idea only remotely connected with that of the main clause.

EXERCISE 26. Independent Elements

Point out each independent element in the following sentences. For obvious reasons, the independent elements in these sentences are not punctuated; but in regular usage they are frequently separated from the rest of the sentence by commas or, when they are long, by dashes. State how you would punctuate each independent element.

1. The procedure to say the least is unusual.
2. We are certain Mr. Webster that the instructions are correct.
3. Yes the instructions are correct.
4. These instructions moreover are complete.
5. Well what are we waiting for?
6. The book that you bought in Chicago I tell you is a valuable first edition.
7. The instructor wants to see you Bob as soon as you have completed your last experiment.
8. In this three-hour course however the class will meet only twice a week.
9. The report you submitted yesterday I am pleased to say is the best that has been written this term.

10. Ah now I have the microscope adjusted so perfectly that I can clearly see the structure of the cell.

11. This experiment we have discovered is much more complicated than we thought it was.

12. After the meeting Mr. Secretary I shall give you a copy of my report.

13. Jerry I warn you that the assignment for tomorrow is long.

14. Anyone who ever went to the top of the peak knows of course that the last fifty yards of the climb is exhausting.

15. No doubt you have heard the news everyone seems to know about it that next Wednesday all classes will be dismissed at noon.

16. The amount of rain we had last night I tell you was not enough to dampen the grass.

17. In this dry season even a little rain is nevertheless better than none.

18. Everybody of course will want to attend the picnic.

19. This washable ink you know is not satisfactory for making permanent records.

20. The opinion of the committee therefore is that the additional cost should be met by increasing the dues.

EXERCISE 27. Independent Elements

Follow the instructions for Exercise 26.

I tell you John that I did not see you. No I do not blame you Maribeth for smiling. I know of course that you do not believe me but I am glad nevertheless that both of you are amused. When I tell you what really happened you will probably laugh. You see I had been standing there a long time sprinkling that large strip of grass between the house and the driveway. With nothing to do but hold the hose you know how monotonous it is I began to think of the flower bed I intended to make there. Oh very well have it your way. No you did not say a word but I do not need much imagination you can be sure to know what you were thinking. I admit that I was merely dreaming. I was seeing that plot of ground that whole long strip neatly cultivated with dozens of rosebushes planted in rows and each bush moreover was covered with roses big plump buds and half-opened flowers ready to be cut. I was not sprinkling grass at all I tell you but a gaily colored rose bed. Believe me or not I saw the flowers distinctly. Furthermore I saw butterflies colored like brilliant calico trembling on the blooms and I saw the bees burrowing into their hearts. There were so many bees that I could in fact hear them hum. I was no doubt getting drowsy. Then suddenly down at the far end that little terrier the one you know with the black spot on his back dashed into the garden and you might say into the midst of my dream. Annoyed I turned the hose at him hoping to drive him away and just at that moment you would have to be coming around the corner of the house. Well that is my story. It does not dry your clothes I must admit but change them now and tomorrow I will have them pressed.

SECTION B

Aspects of the Structure Requiring Special Attention: Phrases and Clauses

127-190 for W 13/58
Friday

Phrases and Dependent Clauses in Building Sentences

1. As you learned in Section A, a sentence is built of words, which are classified according to their use as parts of speech. These words are not thrown together haphazardly; but, as materials are used in the construction of a building, they are arranged according to a design in which each one is related in function to the other words in the sentence. Sometimes these words serve their purpose singly; sometimes, however, they serve in groups. Just as single stones may be fitted together to make a column that then serves as a structural unit in a building, so single words may be related in a group that functions as a structural unit in a sentence. Such units, or groups, are called *phrases* and *clauses*.

2. The fact that you have single words, phrases, and clauses to use in building sentences gives you freedom to express a thought in the clearest and most effective way. In some sentences these units may be used interchangeably without altering the essential thought:

> A four-gabled house
> A house with four gables ⎬ stands on the hill.
> A house that has four gables

> The healthy man
> The man in good health ⎬ can enjoy living.
> The man who is healthy

A sentence, of course, should contain no more words than are needed to express a thought or to produce an effect;

so you should not use a group of words if a single word
will serve the same purpose. But frequently a single word
is inadequate.

He opened the doors of the theater
$\begin{cases} \text{early.} \\ \text{before seven.} \\ \text{before the actors fin-} \\ \quad \text{ished rehearsing.} \end{cases}$

Here the first thought can be expressed with the help of a
one-word adverb, but the second requires a phrase and the
third a clause.

3. You have choices also between different kinds of
phrases and clauses. The use of one rather than another
may produce greater lucidity or emphasis or variety.
Take the following sentence:

> The men going to work in the morning buy apples from
> the old woman selling fruit at Grand Avenue.

The two participial phrases of parallel structure make this
sentence clumsy. It may be improved in various ways;
for example, by changing the first to a prepositional
phrase, "on their way to work in the morning," or by
changing the second to a relative clause, "who sells fruit
at Grand Avenue." Here the result is greater variety.
More important, however, is the proper choice to insure
correct logical relationship of the parts of the sentence.
Take the following statement:

> The motor has been rebored, and I must drive the car
> slowly.

Here we have two coordinate clauses joined by *and*, but
the thoughts are not coordinate, for a cause-and-effect
relationship is clearly implied. The cause should be
stated in a dependent clause rather than a coordinate one:

> Since the motor has been rebored, I must drive the car
> slowly.

4. You can see that a full understanding of these constructions will enable you to make better sentences. Moreover, you should have less trouble with punctuation, since most of the marks are used in connection with phrases and clauses. It is essential, therefore, that you learn how phrases and clauses are put together, how they are fitted into sentences, and how they function in the whole structure.

Proper Use within Sentences

5. First of all, you must recall that phrases and dependent clauses, used as units within sentences, function as parts of speech. They may serve as *nouns, adjectives,* or *adverbs.*

> *To get to the show early* is important.   (Phrase as noun)
> The audience believed *what the speaker said.*   (Dependent clause as noun)
> *Riding the untamed bronco* was thrilling.   (Phrase as noun)
> The chairs *that we made* are still unpainted.   (Dependent clause as adjective)
> The car *parked in the driveway* is mine.   (Phrase as adjective)
> We closed the windows *when the rain began.*   (Dependent clause as adverb)
> Angela is too sleepy *to read the book.*   (Phrase as adverb)

Misuse as Sentences

6. Since phrases and clauses are parts of speech used within sentences, it follows that you must not use them as independent sentences. Those used in the foregoing examples — such as *what the speaker said, riding the untamed bronco,* or *when the rain began* — make no sense when they stand alone. Unrelated to other words in a grammatically complete sentence with a subject and predicate verb, they are mere fragments of thought. They are not sentences. When they are used as such, they are often

referred to as *incomplete sentences;* but generally they are called *fragments*.

7. Some complete statements can be made without the use of all the elements required in a grammatically complete sentence. For example, in imperative sentences the subject is often omitted. In giving a command, a person might say "Leave this house at once!" or "Go!" or "Get out of here!" Though these expressions do not contain a subject, all of them, of course, would be recognized as complete statements — and, consequently, as sentences — because they are conventionally used as sentences. No one has any doubt about their meaning, not merely because the missing part can be supplied readily, but chiefly because it has been supplied by generations of people. In everyday conversation the type of sentence in which not all the elements are expressed is used regularly without any question about the meaning of it; sometimes, in fact, both the subject and predicate are omitted without causing any doubt about the meaning, as the following dialogue illustrates:

"What shall I do?"
"Go!"
"Where?"
"Anywhere."
"New York?"
"Yes."
"Tonight?"
"Why wait? The sooner the better."
"Very well. Goodby."

8. Incomplete sentences of the foregoing type — without either the subject or predicate or both subject and predicate — are called *elliptical sentences.* By actual structure, of course, they are not sentences, since a sentence must have a subject and a predicate. By usage, though, they are sentences, because the necessary missing parts can be readily supplied, and they convey a complete thought.

9. Some writers, however, go beyond this type of sentence. They use phrases and dependent clauses as complete sentences in order to produce certain predetermined effects, such as an informal tone, a feeling of tension, an impression of incoherent or rapid and superficial thinking, or emphasis. These effects, however, are seldom achieved skillfully except by an experienced writer who knows well how to write a complete sentence, but deliberately chooses to employ a fragment. Until you have reached this stage, you should avoid using these incomplete sentences. The reason is not primarily that they are grammatically unfinished, but that they do not make a statement, and so their meaning is not clear. A competent writer knows when they make sense. Until you do also, you would do well to write only grammatically complete sentences.

10. You see, then, that there are two reasons why you should give special attention to phrases and dependent clauses. One is to learn how they are constructed and how they are used properly within a sentence. The other is to avoid misusing them as sentences — that is, to avoid using fragments as sentences. The purpose of the next four Study Units is to help you achieve both of these objectives.

Prepositional Phrases

1. A phrase is any group of related words that does not contain a subject and a predicate. It is not any group of words, you notice, but any group of *related* words — words that in some way belong together, as shown in the following sentences:

> You can find this word *in any dictionary.*
> The book *with the blue cover* is new.
> The men *painting the roof* are sunburned.
> *Sailing a small boat* requires skill.
> Everybody wanted *to see the show.*

Since these groups of related words contain neither subjects nor predicates, they cannot stand alone as sentences. They are structural units in their sentences, serving as parts of speech. For example, *in any dictionary* is an adverbial phrase modifying *can find; with the blue cover* is an adjective phrase modifying *book; painting the roof* is an adjective phrase modifying *men. Sailing a small boat* and *to see the show* are phrases used as nouns; the first is the subject of *requires,* and the second is the object of *wanted.*

2. The name *phrase* can be given to any group of related words not containing a subject and predicate — for example, such a group as *Smith, Jones, and Company* is sometimes called a noun phrase, and a verb consisting of more than one word, such as *has been seen,* may be called a verb phrase. In a more limited sense, however, the word is applied to four types of phrase: *prepositional, participial, gerund,* and *infinitive phrases.* The first of

132

these will be discussed in this Study Unit, the others in the next two Study Units.

Construction of Prepositional Phrases

3. The simple prepositional phrase is easily recognized and understood. It consists of a preposition with its object, which is a substantive — generally a noun or a pronoun. In the immediately preceding sentence, *of preposition* and *with object* are simple prepositional phrases.

4. In most prepositional phrases the object has one or more modifiers, as in *over the fence; across the swollen river; beside the big house with gables; up the long, grass-covered hills that are found in southern Ohio.* In the first two phrases, the object is modified by one or two single words; in the third it is modified by single words and a phrase; and in the fourth it is modified by single words and a clause. These modifiers may in turn have modifiers.

> We drove on the *newly* paved road. (*Paved*, which modifies *road*, is in turn modified by *newly*.)
> We drove on a road *soon* to be opened *to the public*. (*To be opened* modifies *road* and is itself modified by *soon* and *to the public*.)

5. A complete prepositional phrase, then, consists not only of a preposition and its object, but also of all the modifiers of the object and of all the modifiers of the modifiers. In other words, it consists of all the direct and indirect modifiers of the object. These may be words, phrases, or clauses.

6. The following sentences exemplify prepositional phrases with various types of modifiers and various levels of modification:

> We drove on the paved road connecting Joslin and Macron. (*Road* is here modified by the participial phrase *connecting Joslin and Macron.*)

We drove on a paved road in a beautiful valley between high hills. (The complete prepositional phrase, with all direct and indirect modifiers, is *on a paved road in a beautiful valley between high hills. Road*, the object of the simple phrase, is modified by *a, paved*, and the simple phrase *in valley; valley*, in turn, is modified by *a, beautiful*, and *between hills;* and *hills* is modified by *high*.)

We drove on a paved road leading into Macron, which is the largest town in the whole county. (All the words after *We drove* form a complete prepositional phrase. *Road*, the object of the simple phrase, is modified by *a, paved*, and the participial phrase *leading into Macron; Macron*, in turn, is modified by the clause *which is the largest town in the whole county; town*, the predicate noun of the clause, is modified by *the, largest*, and *in county; county* is modified by *the* and *whole*.)

Misuse as Complete Sentence

7. As you can see, the short prepositional phrases are so easily recognized that you are not likely to mistake them for sentences. The long phrases, obviously, are more difficult; but they will cause you no trouble if you remember that a group of words is not a sentence unless it contains a subject and a predicate verb and conveys a complete thought. The kind of phrase you need to watch for is one containing a dependent clause, which must have a subject and a predicate verb:

> The decorator has put new paper *on the ceiling that the water damaged.*

The object of the simple phrase *on ceiling* is modified not only by *the*, but also by the dependent clause *that the water damaged.* Since this clause has a subject and a predicate verb, *water* and *damaged*, you might mistake it for a sentence. But the whole clause, with its introductory connective, is obviously unable to stand alone;

and you should have no trouble in recognizing it as a part of speech within the phrase, an adjective modifier of *ceiling*, itself the object of a prepositional phrase that functions as an adverb modifying *put*.

8. Generally a dependent clause within a prepositional phrase serves as an adjective modifying the object; but sometimes, as a noun clause, it is the object of the preposition.

> You should send the parcel *with whoever is driving his car.*

In this dependent clause, the subject is *whoever* and the predicate verb is *is driving*. The whole clause, functioning as a noun, is the object of *with*.

9. Additional examples of dependent clauses used as parts of speech in prepositional phrases are provided by the following sentences, in which the clauses are italicized:

> We admired the delicate flowers on the plant *that you gave us*. (The dependent clause modifies *plant*, the object of the preposition *on*. The complete prepositional phrase is *on the plant that you gave us*, used as an adjective to modify *flowers*.)

> We bought the car from the salesman *who demonstrated it*. (The dependent clause modifies *salesman*, the object of *from*. Complete prepositional phrase: *from the salesman who demonstrated it*, used as an adverb to modify *bought*.)

> The instructor read my story about the festival *that we attended when we visited Lucerne*. (This prepositional phrase contains two dependent clauses. *Festival*, the object of *about*, is modified by *that we attended*; and *attended* is modified by *when we visited Lucerne*. Complete prepositional phrase: *about the festival that we attended when we visited Lucerne*, used as an adjective to modify *story*.)

> The chairman requested comments from *whoever wanted to speak*. (The dependent noun clause is the object of *from*. Complete prepositional phrase: *from whoever*

wanted to speak, used as an adjective to modify *com-ments.*)

The photographer took the picture by a new method *that he learned abroad.* (The dependent clause modifies *method,* the object of *by.* Complete prepositional phrase: *by a new method that he learned abroad,* used as an adverb modifying *took.*)

EXERCISE 28. Prepositional Phrases

In the following sentences point out each *simple* prepositional phrase, that is, each preposition and its object; then, if the phrase consists of more than a preposition and its object, identify the complete phrase by stating how every other word modifies the object.

1. This book belongs to me.
2. For no good reason he stopped playing.
3. I bought this pen at the bookstore that is on Broad Street.
4. He wrote on both sides of the paper.
5. I left my notebook at home.
6. The trees were bending low under the pressure of the fierce wind that was blowing from the northwest.
7. The house on the southwest corner of Grand and Oak streets was badly damaged by fire.
8. Those letters on my desk must be mailed this afternoon.
9. The picture on the cover of the magazine that I bought yesterday when I was in the bookstore is the most amusing one that I have seen recently.
10. He drove around the sharp curves at a speed that made me shudder.

EXERCISE 29. Prepositional Phrases

Follow the directions for Exercise 28.

The largest crowd of the season was waiting tensely for the opening of the championship football game. Nearly every student, hundreds of townspeople, and visitors from all parts of the state were there. The most eager and the most demonstrative of all, of course, were the students. In the center section of the grandstand they were seated in "yelling formation." On the front seats was a group of about fifty young men in red and white striped coats. Apparently they were chosen for their special ability to make noise. Behind this group were sitting other young men without uniforms. Many of them, however, wore gaily colored sweaters and caps. With this group most of the young men of the student body had been seated. On either side of these men was a section or two of girls. Down upon the ground in front of the men's section were prancing three young men in light-blue flannel coats and white trousers. Each one was holding a large megaphone. The young man in the center had raised his megaphone to his mouth. Few people except those in front of him heard his remarks. Apparently, though, he was giving instructions. Throwing his trumpet to the ground, he stretched his arms high above his head. Simultaneously the entire group of students rose and yelled lustily. All three young men now had thrown aside their megaphones, and, with their arms upstretched, they were weaving their bodies rhythmically from side to side. Suddenly they stood still, and the students became silent and sat down. Within a few minutes, however, someone called out, "Here they come!" Immediately everyone in the crowd stood up and shouted independently, and the three young men with the megaphones danced and jumped and turned somersaults. What had happened? Everyone knows, of course. The home team was trotting down the center of the field.

Exercise 30. Prepositional Phrases

Following the numbers below are groups of words written as sentences, though some are merely prepositional phrases. First, distinguish the prepositional phrases from the sentences. Next, if a phrase should be a part of speech in an adjoining sentence, state what part of speech it is and explain exactly how it serves the sentence.

1. Charles Dickens died in 1870. At the age of fifty-eight years.
2. On the table are three books that you ought to read. Each one is interesting.
3. On the paper that I received last Christmas. I wrote a letter to my cousin.
4. In the magazine that came yesterday is a thrilling story. About a trip to the South Sea Islands in a small yacht.
5. The man paced nervously. Up and down the street.
6. Upon the table that is littered with papers and books. You will find your pencil.
7. This is an old picture of my brother. Upon the desk yonder is his latest picture.
8. They climbed to the top of the mountain. Over the big rocks and through drifts of snow.
9. After we had quit looking, a small boy said that he had found our ball. Behind a little tuft of grass that was growing at the edge of the fairway.
10. The speaker came to the front of the platform. Behind him were twenty-five or thirty men and women who were members of the local committee. In front of him were two thousand people with upturned faces, eagerly waiting for him to begin.

Participial and Gerund Phrases

Nature of a Participial Phrase

1. Like a prepositional phrase, a participial phrase is a group of related words used as a part of speech in a sentence. It serves, however, only as an adjective modifier of a substantive. Since it is a modifier, it cannot stand alone as an independent sentence.

> *Blowing ninety miles an hour*, the wind swept away everything in its path.

In this sentence, the phrase is used as an adjective to modify *wind*. Essentially, the modifier is the participle, *blowing*. All of the other words in the phrase are related to the participle. Since every phrase of this kind is built around a participle, which is one of several verbals, you must first of all understand its nature and function.

Core of the Phrase: the Participle

2. A participle, though used as an adjective, is fundamentally a verb. It thus has two functions. As a verb it indicates action or condition, and so it may have a complement or adverbial modifiers or both. As an adjective it must modify a noun or some word or group of words used as a noun.

3. The various forms of the participle are given in Study Unit 5, paragraph 52. In order to simplify this discussion, the present active participle (for example, *going, seeing, walking*) will be considered chiefly as illustrating

the nature of all participles. Let us see, through this present active form, how the participle performs its dual function.

> The *running* brook babbled over the stones.

In this sentence *running* is obviously a verbal form, because it expresses action; and it is as obviously an adjective, because it states a characteristic of the brook. In this usage, in fact, the participle is equivalent to a pure adjective. Now consider another example:

> The boy, *running*, fell.

Here, as in the preceding sentence, *running* clearly modifies *boy* as a pure adjective would, even though it follows *boy* and is inserted as an explanation of what the boy was doing when he fell. The sentence could be written:

> The *running* boy fell.

Construction of the Participial Phrase

4. Generally, however, participles are used not as pure single-word adjectives but as essential parts of phrases.

PARTICIPLE WITH ADVERBIAL MODIFIERS

5. Since the participle is a form of the verb, it may have adverbial modifiers. In order, for example, to give a fuller explanation of what the boy was doing when he fell, one of the foregoing illustrative sentences might be:

> The boy, running swiftly, fell.
> The boy, running swiftly down the street, fell.

Here the participle, still an adjective modifying *boy*, itself has adverbial modifiers — the single adverb *swiftly* and the adverbial phrase *down the street* — to state how and where the action expressed by the participle took place. The participle and its modifiers constitute a phrase that modifies a substantive just as a single modifier would:

> The swiftly-running-down-the-street boy fell.

Even with many more words added to *running*, the relation of *running* to *boy* would not be changed:

> The boy, running swiftly down the street as if he were being chased, fell.

Here the participle has a clause as well as a phrase and a single-word adverb to modify it.

PARTICIPLE WITH COMPLEMENTS

6. Since a participle is a verb, it may have not only adverbial modifiers, but also an object, a predicate noun, or a predicate adjective.

7. *Objects.* In a simple sentence, the direct object of a verb receives or results from the action of the verb, as in the following sentence:

> The catcher throws the *ball.*

Here *ball* is obviously the object of *throws*, which is the simple predicate of the sentence. Now, if *throws* were changed into a participle, it could no longer be the simple predicate of the sentence, but it could take an object — exactly as it can when it is the simple predicate:

> The catcher, throwing the ball, ran toward the pitcher.

Here the main part of the sentence is *The catcher ran toward the pitcher*, and *throwing the ball* is a participial phrase, of which *throwing* is the participle. As a verb, *throwing* takes the object *ball;* as an adjective, it modifies *catcher* — that is, the catcher is *the throwing catcher*. The participle, however, is not the only word that modifies *catcher*. He is not merely *the throwing catcher*, but also *the throwing-the-ball* catcher. In other words, the participle and its object constitute a phrase that modifies like a single-word adjective.

8. A participle may have not only a direct object, but also any other object that a verb may have.

> The catcher, giving the *umpire* the ball, ran to the pitcher. (Indirect object)
>
> The chairman of the committee, naming James *secretary*, opened the meeting. (Predicate objective)
>
> Charles, sneezing a violent, raucous *sneeze*, made the audience laugh. (Cognate object)

9. A participle may have both an object — direct or any other kind — and adverbial modifiers:

> The catcher, quickly tossing the umpire the ball, ran to the pitcher.

10. *Predicate Noun.* A participle may also have a predicate noun.

11. In a simple sentence, a predicate noun is a substantive that occurs in the predicate as another name for the subject, as in the following sentence:

> Mr. Jones is *president.*

Now, if *is* were changed to its participial form *being*, it could no longer be the simple predicate of the sentence; but it could have a predicate noun, exactly as if it were the simple predicate:

> Mr. Jones, being president, conducted the meeting.

Being president is a participial phrase, modifying *Mr. Jones*.

12. *Predicate Adjective.* Similarly a participle may have a predicate adjective.

13. In a simple sentence a predicate adjective occurs in the predicate, as does a predicate noun, but it modifies the subject:

> The car is *old.*

If *is* were changed to *being*, as in the preceding example, it could no longer be the simple predicate of the sentence, but it could have a predicate adjective:

> The car, being old, was sold for fifty-five dollars.

14. The principal verb, you recall, that joins a subject to its predicate noun or to its predicate adjective is some form of the copula *to be* (*am, is, are, was, were, have been, had been, shall be,* etc.); and so the principal participle that is used with a predicate noun or predicate adjective is *being.* For the few other verbs that may be used as copulas, refer to Study Unit 5, paragraph 3.

15. You understand now that a participle is both a verb and an adjective. In its function as a verb, it may have complements or adverbial modifiers or both. In its function as an adjective, it *must* modify a noun. The participle alone may modify a noun; but when a participle has other words related to it, the entire participial phrase modifies the noun as a unit.

Misuse as Complete Sentence

16. When a participial phrase comes between the subject and the verb of the sentence in which it is a modifier, as in all of the preceding examples, you are not likely to mistake it for an independent sentence. Often, however, the phrase comes at the head of the sentence or at the end; and if it is long, and especially if it contains a clause as a complement or a modifier, you may be in danger of mistaking it for a complete sentence.

> Having learned at last what the teacher wants us to do with the exercises, I can prepare more intelligently for tomorrow's class.
>
> After we had waited impatiently for an hour, we finally saw the airplane gliding gently to the ground as if it weighed no more than a feather.
>
> The batter sprinted toward first base with all the speed he could muster, throwing the bat as he ran.

Students frequently punctuate such participial phrases as complete sentences, especially when the participle is far removed in the sentence from the substantive that it modifies, as in the first and third sentences above. But you are now able to see how the parts of the participial phrase fit together into a unit that serves as an adjective modifying a noun in the sentence; and since it modifies a noun in the sentence it must be a part of the sentence. With this understanding of the structure and function of a participial phrase you will not punctuate the phrase as if it were an independent sentence.

PARTICIPIAL PHRASE AS NOMINATIVE ABSOLUTE

17. There is another type of participial phrase, however, that you are more likely to mistake for an independent sentence, because, instead of modifying a noun in the sentence of which it is a part, it modifies one that does not in itself have any relationship to the sentence. Consider the following sentence:

> The guide *taking the lead*, the small band of explorers ascended the mountain.

The participial phrase, instead of modifying a noun in the main part of the sentence, such as *band*, modifies a noun of its own, *guide*. Sometimes this noun is said to be the subject of the participle. Regardless of what it is called, however, it is independent of the main sentence; that is, taken by itself, it has no grammatical relationship with any word in the main sentence. For this reason it is said to have an absolute construction. Furthermore, since it names something as if it were a subject, it is said to be in the nominative case. It is, then, an independent, or absolute, nominative; and it is therefore called a *nominative absolute*. Since the participial phrase, which is an adjective, modifies the nominative absolute, the whole expression is called a nominative absolute.

18. In this construction, forms of the participle other than the present active are used frequently.

The guide *having taken* the lead, the explorers ascended the mountain.

The arrangements *being* (or *having been*) *completed*, the trip was begun.

Our destination *reached* at last, we made camp.

19. Regardless of the form of the participle, you can readily see that there is no essential distinction between a participial phrase in a nominative absolute and the ordinary participial phrase that was explained in the preceding paragraphs. The only difference is that the ordinary participial phrase modifies a noun in the main sentence, and the participial phrase in a nominative absolute modifies a noun that is grammatically independent of the main sentence.

20. It is important for you to know, however, that though the noun is grammatically independent, the nominative absolute phrase is not. It is definitely a part of the main sentence, serving as an adverb. This relationship is illustrated by comparing the following two sentences:

The guide being gone, the trip was postponed.

Because the guide was gone, the trip was postponed.

The library being closed, we studied at home.

Because the library was closed, we studied at home.

Since this type of phrase belongs to the structure of the main sentence, as much as an ordinary participial phrase, *it is not a separate sentence, and it must not be punctuated as if it were.* Of course, you will not so punctuate it, any more than you will an ordinary participial phrase, if you always keep in mind that a participle — any kind of participle — cannot be used *alone* as the predicate verb of a sentence.

Participle as Part of Predicate Verb

21. Since the foregoing discussion has been concerned with participles and participial phrases as modifiers, you should now recall that, as stated in Study Unit 5, a parti-

ciple may be the predicate verb of a sentence when it is ac-
companied by a suitable form of the auxiliary verb *have*
(*has, have, had, shall* or *will have*) or *be* (*am, is, was, were,
has* or *have been, had been, shall* or *will be*).

22. The past participle, of course, is one of the three
principal parts of the verb, required in all of the perfect
tenses. Used with the auxiliary *have* it expresses active
voice; used with the auxiliary *be*, it expresses passive
voice.

ACTIVE VOICE

Our dog *has run* away.

The birds *have eaten* all of the crumbs.

When the lumber arrived, the carpenters *had* already *gone*.

Tomorrow we *shall have seen* the show three times.

PASSIVE VOICE

I *am* always *seated* by the same usher.

The house *was sold* last week.

The books *have been returned* to the library.

The speech *had* obviously *been memorized*.

The speaker *will* now *be escorted* to the platform.

The building *will have been completed* by the time college
opens.

23. The present active participle may be used in any of
the tenses with the auxiliary verb *be* to express progressive, or continuing, action or condition; the present passive participle may be similarly used in the present and
past tenses.

I *am writing* a short story.

He *was painting* a picture yesterday.

The flags *have been fluttering* in the breeze.

The water lilies *had been growing* rapidly.

We *shall be studying* this chapter all next week.

By the time you arrive tomorrow we *shall have been
working* for an hour.

The work *is being done* by Mr. Jones.

The witness *was being questioned*.

Participial and Gerund Phrases Differentiated

24. In identifying participial phrases and guarding against their use as sentences, you must be sure that you know the difference between a participle and a gerund. Since the two look exactly alike, you can distinguish between them only by knowing how each is used.

25. The most frequently used gerund is the present active. Like the present active participle, it is a form of the verb ending in *ing*. The participle, however, is a form of the verb used as an adjective, and the gerund is a form of the verb used as a noun. Compare, for instance, the following two sentences:

> The boy, *running* down the street, stumbled and fell.
> *Running* is a good exercise for boys.

In the first sentence, *running* is an adjective modifying *boy;* in the second, it is a noun, the subject of the sentence.

26. Since a gerund is a noun, it may have all of the uses of a noun; that is, it may be used as a subject, as an appositive, as the direct or indirect object of a verb, as the object of a preposition, or as a predicate noun:

> *Running* is good exercise. (Subject)
> One healthful exercise, *running*, is too strenuous for old people. (Appositive)
> The speaker praised *running* as a healthful exercise. (Direct object of verb)
> The coach gave *running* first place on his list of healthful exercises. (Indirect object of verb)
> By *running* a mile every day he developed his lungs. (Object of preposition)
> His chief exercise was *running*. (Predicate noun)

27. As a noun, furthermore, a gerund may have adjective modifiers or possessive modifiers.

Long-distance running requires vigor and endurance.
Fast running is likely to cause difficult breathing.
The *boy's* running was improving.
We could see that *his* running was improving.

28. But a gerund is also a verb, and so it may have adverbial modifiers or a complement or both. The gerund and its related words form a gerund phrase, and the whole unit functions as a substantive.

> *Running swiftly for a long time* is exhausting. (The phrase, consisting of the gerund and its adverbial modifiers, is the subject of the sentence.)
> *Lending him the car* was a mistake. (Here the gerund has indirect and direct objects; the whole phrase is the subject of the sentence.)
> *Being a success* is not necessarily *being happy*. (Here the first phrase is the subject and the second the predicate noun of the sentence; in the first the gerund has a predicate noun, in the second a predicate adjective.)

29. A gerund phrase is less likely than a participial phrase to be mistaken for an independent sentence, since as a substantive it is generally essential to the structure of the sentence and is therefore more easily recognized as a part of the sentence. But you should be on your guard with such sentences as the following:

> One sport I enjoy more than any other I have tried — fishing for trout in a mountain stream. (Here the gerund phrase is an appositive so far removed from the noun with which it is in apposition that it might be carelessly mistaken for a separate sentence.)
> Painting pictures having proved not very lucrative, Paul now looked about for some other means of earning a living. (Here the gerund phrase is a nominative absolute modified by a participial phrase; the danger of mistaking such a construction for an independent sentence has been discussed above.)

Even such sentences will not mislead you if you remember that the gerund phrase is a substantive that functions like a single word in the sentence.

30. In summary, then, present participles and gerunds have the following similarities and differences. Both are forms of verbs ending in *ing*. As verbs, both may take complements and have adverbial modifiers. Both, moreover, function as another part of speech: the participles as adjectives; the gerunds as nouns. In this second usage, they are different. Participles, as adjectives, must modify substantives. Gerunds, as nouns, may serve in a sentence wherever nouns may serve; and, in addition to being modified by adverbs, they may be modified by adjectives.

EXERCISE 31. Participial Phrases

Identify each *complete* participial phrase in the following sentences and point out both the participle and the substantive that the participle modifies. As you proceed, state which of the phrases are nominative absolutes.

1. At Minford the main road divides, the north branch going to Otway and the south branch going to Ripley.
2. Stumbling over the rock, he lost his balance and fell.
3. The lake being shallow on our side, we were unable to dive.
4. The bird flew from tree to tree, flitting through the branches like a shadow.
5. The older boys, dividing the work among themselves, prepared the lunch for the picnic, some of them making the sandwiches, others the coffee, and still others the salad.
6. Two sturdy and stately oaks stood before the door, their leaves rustling in the breeze.
7. The berries being ripe, we picked them.
8. Standing on the top of the hill, we could see the village in the far distance.
9. Socrates, Plato, and Aristotle were three Greek philoso-

phers, Socrates being the one who was forced to drink the deadly hemlock.

10. Spreading its black, barren limbs between us and the rising sun, the tree was a ghostly silhouette.

EXERCISE 32. Participles in Phrases and in Predicate Verbs

After each of the following numbers are groups of words punctuated as grammatically complete sentences. Only some of the groups, however, are complete sentences; the others are participial phrases or nominative absolutes. Identify each participial phrase and nominative absolute. If it belongs logically to an adjoining sentence, explain its grammatical relationship. Identify each participle in any of the groups that is a part of a predicate verb, and then state what the complete predicate verb is.

1. We have been sliding down the glacier. The guide showing us how to go.
2. The car being new. We were driving it slowly.
3. Heading the parade were six men on horseback.
4. The river was rising fast. The rain having fallen for six days.
5. Three pictures were hanging on the wall. The largest one being a copy of a painting by Corot.
6. She was rocking monotonously in a creaking, dilapidated chair. At the same time she was staring at something on the other side of the street.
7. Two men were leaning from the fourth-story window. One looking up the street, and the other looking down.
8. The traveler being weary from a long tramp. He was lying asleep beside the road.
9. The bright light on the porch was burning all night. It was illuminating the whole neighborhood.
10. The parade coming down the street. The children were crowding to the curb.

EXERCISE 33. Participles Distinguished
from Gerunds

Identify the participles and gerunds in the following
sentences and state fully the function of each in its sentence.

1. Opening the door quietly, he entered the room.
2. He paced the floor for more than an hour, going from one
   room to another.
3. The middle room being spacious, he paused a moment.
4. Then, walking to the other side of the room, he indifferently pushed the door shut.
5. He stepped slowly to the middle of the room, standing
   under the large chandelier.
6. Several times he took a step or two, but he did not resume
   his monotonous pacing.
7. Hearing the creak of a hinge behind him, he stopped suddenly; but he did not turn around.
8. Looking into the mirror, he saw the door swinging open
   slowly.
9. It stopped against the wall, causing a delicate vibration.
10. The slight swaying of the chandelier and the gentle fluttering of the curtain — the latter being at the window
    opposite him — indicated that a breeze was rushing in.
11. Suddenly he turned about face, expecting to meet an intruder.
12. His hands clenched, he stepped forward.
13. Entering the room, however, was nothing but the breeze.
14. Going to the door and looking into the next room were
    tasks of a moment.
15. The outside door standing open, the breeze through the
    room was strong.
16. Table covers, cards, and sheets of music were scattered
    over the floor, all of them having been blown by the
    wind.
17. He remembered that the door was open when he came,
    the afternoon being unusually warm.

18. No one being in the room, he could not understand how the inside door had been opened.
19. Feeling something rubbing his ankles, he looked down.
20. There at his feet was the family cat, purring and looking up at him.

EXERCISE 34.   Participles Distinguished from Gerunds

Follow the instructions for Exercise 33.

Late one afternoon, after we had traveled nearly a week, my partner and I arrived at a large ranch where we expected to find work for the summer. We were tired and hungry. Being young, we easily threw off the fatigue, but not the hunger. Our eating, in fact, had given us most of our anxiety. Having big appetites and little money, we had to struggle constantly with ourselves to keep from spending too much for food. On the train we were able to control ourselves, because sitting day and night in a stuffy day coach is enough to take the appetite from even the most robust person. The last seven miles of our trip, however, we had traveled in a light open wagon drawn by two spirited horses. These were the best that we were able to hire at the little town where we had to get off the train. The jolting and swaying of the wagon as we bumped over the road, together with the stimulating air, made us so hungry that we were scarcely able to wait for the next meal. What troubled us now was that we did not see any place to eat. Apparently no room used for dining was connected with the "bunk house," where we had been told to stay until the foreman of the ranch came in.

We waited for him until six o'clock; then my partner, thinking that we probably had been overlooked, announced impatiently that he intended to find someone. As soon as we had stepped outside, we heard a rumbling that sounded as if wagons were coming toward us. Going to the corner of the building we saw three of them approaching the barn. Each held four or five men. One man was driving and the others were sitting on either side and at the rear. Those at the rear were leading extra horses. When they came in front of the barn they stopped and began to unload the wagons and un-hitch the horses. Singling out the one whom we took to be the foreman, we approached him warily and introduced ourselves. In greeting us, he was gruff; but he was much more cordial than we had any right to expect, especially since he was supervising the unhitching and feeding of the horses. When this work was finished, he asked us to go with him and the other men to what was called the "mess hall." It was not really a hall, but a large room in the foreman's house. Where it was, we did not care; we saw only the long tables that were actually loaded with food. For the first time in a week we had all that we wanted to eat.

Infinitive Phrases

1. An infinitive phrase is a group of related words that may serve as any one of three parts of speech, as *noun*, *adjective*, or *adverb*. It is thus only a part of a sentence and cannot stand alone as a sentence. Since this phrase is built around an infinitive, you must first understand the nature and function of this core of the phrase.

Core of the Phrase: the Infinitive

INFINITIVE AS VERB

2. In its simplest form, the infinitive corresponds to the first person, present tense, singular number of the verb, such as *go*, *walk*, *do*, and *see*. (*Be* is the only exception.) Generally it is preceded by *to*, which is called the *sign of the infinitive*, as in *to go* or *to walk*. This *to*, however, must not be confused with the preposition, which has a substantive as an object. It is part of the verbal. Even when it is omitted, as explained later, it is "understood."

3. An infinitive has the following forms:

ACTIVE VOICE

	PRESENT TENSE	PERFECT TENSE
Simple	to see	to have seen
Progressive	to be seeing	to have been seeing

PASSIVE VOICE

Simple	to be seen	to have been seen

4. As this table shows, only in the simple present does the *to* come immediately before the word that expresses the main verbal idea. In all other forms this main idea is expressed by a present or past participle, which is preceded by *to be*, *to have been* (the perfect tense of *to be*), or *to have*.

5. The use of the various forms is illustrated in the following sentences:

> We intend *to see* you next week.
> We are glad *to have seen* you again.
> We hope *to be seeing* the yacht races at this time next week.
> It is pleasant *to have been seeing* our old friends here.
> You are tall enough *to be seen* anywhere.
> This set of pictures was *to have been seen* before the others.

Not one of these sentences, you see, would be complete without the predicate verbs *intend*, *are*, *hope*, *is*, *are*, *was*. They, not the infinitives, are the verbs of the sentences. The infinitives are merely parts of speech within the sentences.

6. *Infinitive without* to. In two types of structure the sign of the infinitive is omitted.

7. One is that in which the infinitive is preceded by the auxiliaries *shall*, *will*, *should*, *would*, *can*, *could*, *must*, *may*, *might*, *do*, or *did:*

> We shall *go* with you.
> I should *fall* if I tried to skate.
> You may *go* when you have completed your work.
> I know that he did *ring* the bell.

Though these designated words are infinitives without *to*, they ought to be considered as belonging with the auxiliaries to form predicate verbs, as in *shall go* and *should fall*.

8. Another structure is that in which the predicate verb is *see*, *hear*, *feel*, *dare*, or *make:*

I saw the boy *skate* on the weaving ice.
We heard the motor *purr*.
I felt the house *shake* in the wind.
We dare not *skate* on this thin ice.
The play was so sad that it made me *cry*.

The italicized words are not a part of the verb, but are infinitives with *to* understood.

INFINITIVE AS NOUN, ADJECTIVE, OR ADVERB

9. An infinitive may function in a sentence as a noun, an adjective, or an adverb.

10. As a *noun*, an infinitive may be used as any one of the several parts of a sentence for which a noun is used — that is, as *subject, object of a verb, object of a preposition, predicate noun*, or *appositive:*

To run will not help now.   (Subject of *will help*)
I want *to run*.   (Object of *want*)
I have no choice except *to run*.   (Object of the preposition *except*)
His first impulse was *to run*.   (Predicate noun)
His first impulse, *to run*, was checked.   (Appositive, in apposition with *impulse*)

11. As an *adjective*, an infinitive modifies a noun in the sentence:

His effort *to run* was useless.   (Modifies *effort*.)
He has had no opportunity *to study*.   (Modifies *opportunity*.)

12. As an *adverb*, an infinitive modifies an adjective, a verb, or another adverb in the sentence:

He was eager *to run*.   (Modifies an adjective *eager*.)
He was urged *to run*.   (Modifies the verb *was urged*.)
He is too tired *to run*.   (Modifies the adverb *too*.)

Construction of the Infinitive Phrase

13. Since an infinitive is a verb as well as a noun, adjective, or adverb, it may have any one or all of the essential characteristics of a verb. It may be modified by an adverb, which may consist of *one word*, a *phrase*, or a *clause;* if its meaning allows, it may have a complement — that is, an *object*, a *predicate noun*, or a *predicate adjective;* and it may have a special kind of subject, as explained later. Its relationship to adverbial modifiers and complements is illustrated in the following sentences.

INFINITIVE WITH ADVERBIAL MODIFIERS

14. An infinitive may have as adverbial modifiers single-word adverbs, phrases, and clauses.

> He always tried to drive *carefully*.
> He wanted to ride *with us*.
> He intended to leave *when his car was repaired*.

INFINITIVE WITH COMPLEMENTS

15. *Objects.* An infinitive may have any of the objects that another verb may have.

> He wanted to help *us*. (Direct object)
> The salesman tried to sell *us* a new *car*. (Both direct and indirect objects)
> John asked the chairman to appoint *him delegate*. (Direct object and predicate objective)
> The little boys wanted to run a *race*. (Cognate object)

16. *Predicate Noun.* The infinitive *to be* may be followed by a predicate noun or pronoun, which is in the nominative case, as are other predicate nouns.

> John tried hard to be a good *student*.
> The sturdiest athlete seems to be *he*.

17. *Predicate Adjective.* The infinitive *to be* and other copulatives, such as *to seem* and *to sound*, may be followed by a predicate adjective.

> The judges tried to be *impartial.*
> The music now begins to sound *familiar.*

INFINITIVE WITH BOTH COMPLEMENTS AND MODIFIERS

18. An infinitive may have both complements and adverbial modifiers, and they in turn may have modifiers of their own, as in the following sentences:

> He made a promise to pay us when he received his money.
> He is willing to be toastmaster at the banquet in honor of the mayor.
> We decided to wear the new gaily colored coats that were given to us last Christmas when we were in Europe.

The whole phrase, no matter how long and complex, still serves in the sentence as a single part of speech — in the preceding sentences as adjective, adverb, and noun, respectively.

INFINITIVE PHRASE WITH INTRODUCTORY WORDS

19. Sometimes an infinitive is introduced by *how, when, where, which,* or some similar word, which is used as a connective in the phrase much as it might be used in a dependent clause. *When such a word comes immediately before the infinitive,* as in the following examples, it is a part of the phrase.

> My brother does not know *how to drive the car.*
> *What to do with used cars* is still an unsolved problem.
> We did not know *where to look next.*

These italicized groups, you see, are used as nouns, exactly as if they were dependent noun clauses.

20. An infinitive may have a subject; but when it does, the subject is always in the objective case, as in the following sentence:

> We asked him to drive us home.

The object of *asked* is not merely *him*, but *him to drive us home*, which is an expression equivalent to a dependent clause, as in *We asked that he drive us home.* It should be thought of, however, as an infinitive phrase that contains a subject.

21. This type of phrase may be the object of a preposition as well as the object of a verb, as in the following examples:

> We waited for *him to come.*
> Her parents arranged for *her to attend the state university*.

The object of *for* is not merely *him* or *her*, but the entire phrase.

22. Even with a subject, an infinitive is not a predicate verb; so the phrase of which it is the core cannot be used as a sentence.

Infinitive Phrase as Nominative Absolute

23. The type of infinitive phrase that you are most likely to mistake for a sentence is one that resembles the nominative absolute that was discussed in connection with the participle. The phrase might be called the nominative absolute with an infinitive. In structure it is the same as a nominative absolute with a participle, except that an infinitive takes the place of the participle, as in the following examples:

> The course will be given next quarter, *the hour to be decided later.*
> A total of fifteen thousand dollars in prizes will be awarded to the five highest contestants, *the first prize to be five thousand dollars.*

24. In order to use this kind of phrase properly, then, you should keep in mind that it consists of an infinitive plus all of the words related to it, and that it must serve as a noun, an adjective, or an adverb. Thus it is a structural unit within a sentence. It is never a sentence.

Exercise 35. Infinitives and Infinitive Phrases

Point out all the infinitives in the following sentences. If an infinitive is the core of an infinitive phrase, identify the complete phrase and show how its parts are related to the infinitive. Then explain how each infinitive or infinitive phrase is used in the sentence as a noun, an adjective, or an adverb.

1. These saplings will grow to be trees.
2. We asked him to give us tickets to the show.
3. The books that you are expected to take with you are on the table.
4. The car that I thought to be new had been driven five thousand miles.
5. The men whom we asked to go with us are here.
6. The boys by whom we expected to be met have been delayed.
7. The method to be followed in this experiment is simple.
8. I expected my partner to be him.
9. The chairman of the entertainment committee invited my brother to participate in the chess tournament.
10. The best chess player in the club seems to be he.
11. The black horse was too awkward to win the race.
12. The visit to the coal mine was more exciting than we expected it to be.
13. The books to be read this month are on the reserve shelf.
14. Will you come to visit me next summer?
15. We requested the manager of the team to telephone us when the game was over.

16. The road for you to travel over is farther south.
17. That is the player whom I thought to be captain.
18. The committee brought enough flowers to provide each girl with three.
19. The young man who is explaining the exhibits to that group of people seems to be the guide.
20. I am pleased to have met you.

[handwritten: Infinitive — an economic way of the clause as takes the place of the clause]

EXERCISE 36. Infinitives and Infinitive Phrases

[handwritten: elliptical phrase.]

Follow the instructions for Exercise 35.

Late one afternoon, after we had traveled nearly a week, my partner and I arrived at a large ranch where we expected to find work for the summer. We were tired and hungry. Being young, we easily threw off the fatigue, but not the hunger. Our eating, in fact, had given us most of our anxiety. Having big appetites and little money, we had to struggle constantly with ourselves to keep from spending too much for food. On the train we were able to control ourselves, because sitting day and night in a stuffy day coach is enough to take the appetite from even the most robust person. The last seven miles of our trip, however, we had traveled in a light open wagon drawn by two spirited horses. These were the best that we were able to hire at the little town where we had to get off the train. The jolting and swaying of the wagon as we bumped over the road, together with the stimulating air, made us so hungry that we were scarcely able to wait for the next meal. What troubled us now was that we did not see any place to eat. Apparently no room used for dining was connected with the "bunk house," where we had been told to stay until the foreman of the ranch came in.

We waited for him until six o'clock; then my partner, thinking that we probably had been overlooked, announced impatiently that he intended to find someone. As soon as we had stepped outside, we heard a rumble that sounded as if wagons were coming toward us. Going to the corner of the building we saw three of them approaching the barn. Each held four or five men. One man was driving and the others were sitting on either side and at the rear. Those at the rear were leading extra horses. When they came in front of the barn they stopped and began to unhitch the horses and unload the wagons. Singling out the one whom we took to be the foreman, we approached him warily and introduced ourselves. In greeting us, he was gruff; but he was much more cordial than we had any right to expect, especially since he was supervising the unhitching and feeding of the horses. When this work was finished, he asked us to go with him and the other men to what was called the "mess hall." It was not really a hall, but a large room in the foreman's house. What it was, we did not care; we saw only the long tables that were actually loaded with food. For the first time in a week we had all that we wanted to eat.

EXERCISE 37. Infinitive Phrases Distinguished from Complete Sentences

The following groups of words are punctuated as sentences, but some of them are only infinitive phrases. Point out each group that is only a phrase, and incorporate it in a complete sentence of your own making. Then point out the infinitives in all the groups, whether phrases or sentences.

1. I plan to go home for lunch.
2. To write an interesting article about taxation problems requires hard work.
3. To read rapidly and intelligently so that you are able to understand and remember.
4. We hope to drive to Lincoln, Nebraska, when this storm is over.
5. His attempt to make an airplane that would be sturdy enough to fly across the ocean without even the slightest engine trouble.

6. He was sensible enough to drive his new car carefully over the rough road that led to the little house on top of the hill.

7. The director announced that several good speakers were to be in town within ten days of each other, the first one to come October 10.

8. When he began to wind the clock, the spring broke.

9. A car was to leave the depot every ten minutes, the first to go at eight o'clock.

10. He did not know how to make a kite.

11. The large cities to be visited before the towns were inspected.

12. The towns to be inspected were not shown on the map.

13. We instructed our guide to go slowly over the narrow, rocky road.

14. Whenever Jack was speaking before an audience, he never knew what to do with his hands.

15. We tried to teach him how to use a dictionary.

16. The teacher told him to study more diligently.

17. For him to give the commencement address in the high school auditorium next Friday night at eight o'clock.

18. His friends could not make him go to the dance.

19. When he tried to smoke, he made himself sick.

20. We left our part of the entertainment for him to plan.

Exercise 38. Phrases Distinguished from Sentences

The groups of words after each of the following numbers are punctuated as sentences, though some of them are only phrases. Point out each group that is only a phrase, and then identify it as prepositional, participial, or infinitive.

1. We have been going to some place in the South each year since 1920. Thus getting away from the extreme cold of our own state.

2. John looked up every word that he did not fully understand. Thus he was constantly increasing his vocabulary.

3. How we were to find the house, we did not know. My brother having lost the address.

4. With its long, low body, its pointed radiator, and its sloping windshield. The car looked as if it had been built for racing.

5. When I saw Mary this morning, she was going to your house with two or three books under her arm. One of them, I noticed, being a large copy of *Gulliver's Travels* that had a beautiful blue binding.

6. No one would object to the heat if the humidity were low.

7. Fred was determined to make high grades. In chemistry and zoology especially.

8. Every day he walked three miles to college and three miles back home. Going and coming in good weather and bad, wading through dust, plowing through snow, and mushing through slush and mud, he never complained. Eager to get an education.

9. Father subscribed for two magazines. One to be given to me as a Christmas present.

10. The teacher asked him to read the first stanza.

11. We are expected to work twenty-five problems this week. Ten of them are to be handed in tomorrow.

12. Jane read three books in two days. The first one being a hundred pages longer than the others, she gave one day to it.

13. To start the motor after the battery had given out, I pushed the car for nearly a quarter of a mile.

14. All of us were sitting in the living room in front of the fireplace. The lights were out. Only the fire illuminating our faces. Then someone began to tell a story.

15. The night was dark. A thick, black blanket hid all the stars. Not a glimmer of light came from any window. Even the several dingy street lamps being out. Yet we were able to see the outline of a horse and rider approaching us.

16. The day being bitter cold, we were able to keep warm only by skating energetically. Usually from one side of the lake to the other, and back again.

17. Although I did not expect any letters, several came to-day. One being from Uncle Charles, whom I had not seen for ten years.

18. After the band came a long line of marchers, followed by another band. The next to come were beautiful floats, representing the various organizations of the city.

19. Delegates came from every state in the Union. The first to arrive being two young men from southwestern Texas.

20. Through the long night we wandered over the slope of the mountain, hoping to find a path that would lead to shelter. With the coming of dawn we found a deserted, one-room cabin. Hidden behind a cluster of tall, bushy pine trees. Here we made a fire to warm ourselves, and then we lay down to sleep.

Dependent Clauses

1. A dependent clause, like a phrase, is a group of related words that functions as a part of speech within a sentence, much as if it were a single word. Since it contains a subject and a predicate verb, you are more likely to mistake it for a complete sentence than to mistake a phrase for one. For this reason you must be especially sure to understand that it is not a complete sentence, but only a part of a sentence.

2. It is true that some writers punctuate dependent clauses — and also phrases and words — as if they were sentences, but even these writers, though some are experienced and skilled, often produce writing that is exceedingly difficult reading. While you are gaining experience, therefore, you should never punctuate a dependent clause, or any other fragment, as if it were a sentence. In order to guard against this possibility you must, of course, learn the characteristics of clauses, so that you can distinguish a dependent from an independent, coordinate, or main clause. In other words, you must know which clauses are able to stand alone as grammatically complete sentences, and which are grammatical parts of other clauses.

The Three Types of Clauses

3. It will be helpful at this point to review briefly the nature of independent, coordinate, and subordinate clauses. Consider first the following group of words:

We have summarized the book.

Since this group, with a subject and a predicate, expresses all of one thought that the writer wants to express, and since it is clear and grammatically complete, it is called an independent clause. Thus it is capable of standing alone as a sentence; and since it is a single clause, it is a simple sentence.

4. If the purpose of a sentence is to show comparison, contrast, or a sequence of action, two or more independent clauses may be joined together by *and, but, or*, or *nor* without changing the status of either as an independent clause that is *capable* of standing alone. Consider, for example, the following sentence:

We have read the book, and now we are summarizing it.

The division into two sentences is possible only because the compound sentence is made up of two independent clauses, both of which are equally important. Each clause is capable of standing alone as the expression of a single complete thought, but in order to show a close relationship between the acts of reading and of summarizing the book, the two thoughts are put into one sentence and are tied together by *and*. What you should note particularly is that these clauses, though joined by a conjunction, are not dependent upon each other. The thoughts that they express are equally important, and so the clauses have the same value; in other words, they are said to be *coordinate*.

5. Many sentences, however, consist of two or more clauses that are not equally important. This is the type to which you should give especial attention, because it contains the dependent clauses that you are likely to mistake for a complete sentence. An example of this type is the following:

We summarized the book because it is long.

The two clauses, of course, are:

We summarized the book. It is long.

Judging only by structure, you can see that each clause is a complete sentence, each containing a subject and a predicate. The clauses, however, are not coordinate, because when they are written as separate sentences they do not express the same thought as that of the original. Neither would they do so if they were made into a compound sentence by being joined with a coordinate conjunction, as the following illustration clearly shows:

We have summarized the book, and it is long.

6. The reason is that one thought depends upon the other for its meaning, and so the whole thought is not expressed unless the two clauses are taken together in their proper relationship. When they are thus together, they obviously are not equal. The first contains the important, or main, thought; and the second contains a less important, or subordinate, thought. The one that contains the main thought, therefore, is called the *main clause;* and the other is called the *subordinate*, or *dependent*, clause.

Characteristics of a Dependent Clause

7. The sentence that we have been examining,

We summarized the book *because it is long,*

reveals the following characteristics of a dependent clause:

   a. It contains a subject and a predicate.
   b. It functions as a part of speech.
   c. It includes a subordinate connective, which is generally the first word of the clause.

SUBJECT AND PREDICATE

8. The requirement that a dependent clause must have a subject and predicate distinguishes it from a phrase, but not from other types of clauses. Every clause must have a subject and a predicate.

PART OF SPEECH

9. The second requirement, that a dependent clause must serve as a part of speech, is shared by dependent clauses and phrases, and distinguishes them from independent and coordinate clauses.

10. A dependent clause may function as an adverb, an adjective, or a noun.

11. A dependent adverbial clause modifies a verb, an adjective, or an adverb — exactly as a single adverb would modify it.

> The game began *when the referee blew his whistle.* (Modifies the verb *began.*)
>
> She is stronger *than she looks.* (Modifies the adjective *stronger.*)
>
> He spoke so suddenly *that we were all startled.* (Modifies the adverb *so.*)

12. A dependent adjective clause modifies a noun or pronoun just as a single adjective would modify it.

> I live in the house *that has the green roof.* (Modifies the noun *house.*)
>
> The flower *that she is wearing* came from my garden. (Modifies the noun *flower.*)
>
> He accomplishes most *who plans most carefully.* (Modifies the pronoun *he.*)

13. A dependent noun clause may be used in any part of a sentence in which a noun or pronoun may be used. It may be used as subject, as appositive, as object of verb or preposition, or as predicate noun. In the following sentences, the dependent clauses are italicized:

> *That the book has not been used* is obvious. (Subject)
>
> The assignment in history, *that we outline the first chapter,* was made at the beginning of the class. (Appositive)
>
> We heard at once *that the game had started.* (Object of verb)

There was no reason for the failure of the experiment except *that we were not careful.* (Object of preposition)

You may give the book to *whoever is in the library.* (Object of preposition)

This kind of paper is *what we want.* (Predicate noun)

The reason for these loose pages is *that the book is old.* (Predicate noun)

CONNECTIVE

14. You see that each of the foregoing sentences consists not only of two clauses, but also of a word that clearly marks one clause as subordinate. This word is called the *connective,* which is considered a part of the dependent clause. Generally it comes at the head of its clause, but in relative clauses it often comes within the clause, as the following sentences show:

I know the man *with* **whom** *you were talking.*

This is the tree *from* **which** *we picked the big red apples.*

15. The connective in an adjective or adverbial clause joins the dependent clause definitely to the word that the clause modifies; but the connective in a noun clause merely introduces the dependent clause, because this type, being such a part of a sentence as subject or object, cannot be joined to a word in a sentence as can a modifying element. Sometimes, however, it is said to join the clause to the verb or to the preposition. The following sentences illustrate the function of connectives:

The car *that has wire wheels* is mine. (*That* connects the clause with *car.*)

The game began *when the referee blew his whistle.* (*When* connects the clause with *began.*)

The student *who makes the highest grade* will be given a book. (*Who* joins the clause to *student.*)

We heard the bell *as we were leaving the house.* (*As* joins the clause to *heard.*)

If our train is on time, we shall arrive at ten o'clock.   (*If* joins the clause to *shall arrive.*)

That the book has not been used is obvious.   (*That* merely introduces the noun clause, which is the subject of the sentence.)

We heard at once *that the game had started.*   (*That* introduces the noun clause, which is the object of the verb *heard.*)

16. The connectives that introduce subordinate clauses have been listed in Study Unit 9, but the most common may profitably be given here:

that	before	whenever
so that	till	whence
in order that	after	whither
although	as though	how
though	unless	while
if	since	who
because	whether	whoever
as	where	which
as if	wherever	whichever
why	whereas	what
until	when	whatever

17. You should note that some of these words are used with independent as well as dependent clauses. *Who, which, what, where, when, whence, whither, how,* and *why* may introduce independent or coordinate clauses that ask a question, as in the following sentences:

Who are you and what do you want?

Where are you going?

When did he come?

Why are you going?

How do you know where I am going?   (The main clause, introduced by *how,* contains a dependent clause, the object of *do know,* which is introduced by the connective *where.*)

How do you know how old I am? (The main clause, introduced by *how*, contains a dependent clause, the object of *do know*, which is introduced by the same word
used as a connective.)

18. A few of the connectives might confuse you because
each of them can be either a subordinate connective or a
preposition. These are *since, until (till), before,* and *after.*
If they are prepositions, of course, they introduce phrases
instead of clauses. You can see the difference in the following illustrations of each use:

We have not been in New York *since* 1920. (Phrase)
We have not been in New York *since* the bridge across
the Hudson River was built. (Clause)
You should not leave *until* tomorrow. (Phrase)
You should not leave *until* your brother comes home.
(Clause)
He stood *before* the fireplace. (Phrase)
He stood for five minutes *before* he said a word. (Clause)
After lunch we went driving. (Phrase)
After we had eaten our lunch, we went driving. (Clause)

19. *That* has four uses. In two of these — as a demonstrative pronoun or a demonstrative adjective — it can,
of course, be used in various positions in both independent
and dependent clauses. But it also has two different functions in introducing subordinate clauses. It may be a
relative pronoun introducing an adjective clause, or it
may be a subordinate conjunction introducing a noun
clause.

We live in the house that has green shutters. (Relative
pronoun, used as subject of dependent clause.)
We live in the house that you saw on the corner. (Relative
pronoun, object of verb in dependent clause.)
That he ought to win the race is admitted by everyone.
(Subordinate conjunction introducing noun clause that
functions as subject of sentence.)

He wrote that he would arrive on the morning train.
(Subordinate conjunction introducing noun clause that
functions as direct object of sentence.)

20. Some subordinate clauses are exceptions to the rule
that every such clause must have a connective.   Occasionally, when the meaning is entirely clear, a relative
pronoun in the objective case or the conjunction *that* is
omitted, as illustrated in the following pairs of sentences:

The plans *that we drew for the house* were much altered.
The plans *we drew for the house* were much altered.
The actor *whom you liked* is not in the cast.
The actor *you liked* is not in the cast.
I knew *that you would come.*
I knew *you would come.*
I found *that I could come after all.*
I found *I could come after all.*

This omission, when it is permissible, sometimes helps to
avoid awkwardness when a connective similar to the one
omitted must be used in the same sentence.   Notice how
much smoother the following sentence becomes when the
first *that* is omitted:

The contractor altered the plans *that* we chose for the
house *that* is being built next door.

One Dependent Clause as Member of Another

21. Thus far we have been examining dependent clauses
that are related to main clauses.   But a dependent clause
may have another dependent clause related to it as a part
of speech, either a substantive or a modifier, and hence
indirectly related to the main clause.   We may call a dependent clause that is directly related to the main clause a
primary dependent clause, and one that is related to a
primary dependent clause a *secondary* dependent clause.
Similarly a secondary dependent clause may have a *tertiary* dependent clause.   All dependent clauses, however,

are ultimately related, directly or indirectly, to the main clause.

22. In the following sentences the rank of the subordinate clauses is indicated by the numeral above the first word of each.

> The instructor said *that we may write on any subject that interests us.*
>
> The agent *who called while you were away* requested *that you see him when you returned.*
>
> On Wednesday morning, *after we had had a good breakfast,* we drove west from Raton, a small town in northern New Mexico, *where we stayed two days while our car was being repaired.*
>
> The class became quiet *when the instructor announced that he would excuse all students who could answer his first question.*
>
> *What the instructor said before you came in* was *that we may leave when we have solved all the problems that he assigned yesterday.*

Summary

23. Remember that the parts of a sentence you are likely to mistake for complete sentences are the following:

> Phrases
>> Prepositional
>> Participial
>> Gerund
>> Infinitive
> Dependent Clauses

Look out for these! Remember that they are not sentences, but only parts. When required at all, they complete the thought of a statement. For this reason they belong to the sentence of which they are a part of the thought. This sentence — any sentence — must have at least a subject and a predicate verb, and it must be able to stand alone as the expression of a complete thought.

Exercise 39. Dependent Clauses Distinguished from Main Clauses

Point out every complete dependent clause in the following sentences and state how it is used in its sentence, whether as a noun, an adjective, or an adverb. If a complete clause contains more than one dependent clause, identify each as primary, secondary, tertiary, etc., and then state how each is related to the clause of which it is a part.

1. We shall eat when the coffee is ready.
2. This is the hat I want.
3. All of the houses on the west side of the street, except the one on the corner, are alike.
4. What we were told was that the factory would resume work tomorrow.
5. The chairman went before the disorderly crowd and demanded that everyone be silent while the speaker was talking.
6. We went in bathing every day so that we could get well tanned.
7. Who will dive after this coin if I throw it into the water?
8. Where did you go after I left you?
9. Nibbling industriously at a piece of apple, a little chipmunk was sitting upon a rock when we arrived.
10. When we were in Berlin last year, we heard several of the operas that were written by Wagner, who, as you have been told, is one of the best-known German composers.

11. After five hours of driving through mud, we were worn out; but we were not too tired to eat a big meal before we went to bed.
12. Which road shall we take when we leave tomorrow?
13. The president of the class wanted to know who would go to the picnic.
14. That was the best game of the season.
15. That Lord Bacon was a brilliant man is indisputable.
16. From the time that we were in the third grade, we read the best books that we could get.
17. I do not know how we shall be able to give the play without making more scenery.
18. As the train went around the curve, the engineer blew the whistle, and then he quickly closed the throttle.
19. Who are those students that are climbing the mountain?
20. Those tall spires that were common on churches fifty years ago, even on the small ones, are seldom seen today.

EXERCISE 40.   Identification of Dependent Clauses

Follow the directions for Exercise 39.

On a recent automobile trip over the Rocky Mountains we found ourselves in a situation that we met in an unusual manner.   Leaving home about ten o'clock in the morning, we planned to drive to a mountain resort so that we could stay all night in a small cabin, which we had already engaged. Knowing that most of our bedding would be furnished, we had taken with us only a few blankets for each person.   If we had faintly suspected that we might have to sleep outside, we should have taken more, because we knew from experience how cold a September night can be at an altitude of nine thousand feet.   That experience was what caused us to reserve the cabin.   The roads were rougher than we had expected, and darkness overtook us by the time that we arrived at a small, straggly settlement fifteen miles from our destination. Being too tired to drive over rough mountain roads in the dark, we decided to try in this little town to rent a cabin in which we could sleep for the night and cook our supper and breakfast.

As we came into the town, which consisted of only a couple dozen houses and a few stores, we thought that we saw some vacant cabins; but after we had gone from store to store inquiring for one, we began to think that we had been mistaken. Then we first had visions of ourselves lying out under the stars with only a couple of thin blankets over us. At the last store, however, we were fortunate enough to rent, not a cabin, but a five-room, two-story house that was set apart from the other houses at the edge of town. As you might expect, our spirits began to rise at once — especially after we had been told that the house was completely furnished.

When we saw it, though, we were disappointed. It was completely furnished, even to kitchen utensils, but it was so untidy and musty that we never could have slept or eaten in it. What we were to do, we did not know. Unfortunately, we already had paid our rent, and we did not like to lose the money. No doubt we did wrong in paying before we had seen the place, but the scarcity of any kind of shelter made us eager to secure this chance. Naturally, we felt as if we had thrown our money away. It was now too dark to look elsewhere or to go on, and we were hungry and tired.

In our inspection we had observed that, though the house was dirty, the mattresses on the beds were clean; so someone suggested that we could escape the odor of the house and still keep ourselves off the cold ground by taking the mattresses out into the back yard and sleeping there. No other house being close to ours, all of us thought that the proposal was a good one, and so we dragged the mattresses outside, laid them beside the car, and made our bed for the night. Then we built a fire and cooked our supper. After we had eaten our fill and had drunk several cups of hot black coffee apiece, we lay down under the stars to sleep.

Apparently, however, we had been dozing only a short time when we were wakened by the frantic barking of dogs, the bellowing of cows, and the irregular clanking of cowbells. All of us sat up, startled by the bedlam. In our half-sleep we thought that the whole world had gone mad; but we soon discovered that some dogs were chasing cows in a circle about our house. As soon as we were widely enough awake to take in the situation, one of our group threw rocks at the dogs until they ran away. When we lay down again, however, sleep was gone. The moon had risen and was shining in our faces; and the cold had begun to come through our thin blankets. Some bravely tried to sleep, but the rest of us built up the fire and sat around it until dawn.

Those who never have gone through an uncomfortable night cannot know how relieved we were when we saw the first glimmer of day. Though still sleepy and tired, we were so eager to leave the place that we quickly put our blankets into the car and returned the mattresses that we had taken from the house. We should have driven away immediately if we had not discovered that the water in our coffee can, which had stood beside the fire for several hours, was hot. We decided, then, to eat breakfast. As soon, though, as we had eaten a bite and had drunk a cup or two of hot coffee, we left for the place where we should have been.

Exercise 41. Parts of Sentences Distinguished from Complete Sentences

Of the following groups of words after each number, some are complete sentences and some are only phrases or dependent clauses. Identify each group that is not a complete sentence by stating which kind of phrase or clause it is. If it could be a logical part of an adjoining sentence, state how it should be related to the sentence.

1. An electric fan keeping the air of the room in motion. We were able to sleep through the hot night.
2. Jane could not attend classes yesterday. Because she had a very bad cold.

3. This term you are to hand in five papers. Which are to be neatly typewritten.

4. In most colonial churches the men and women attending the services were separated. The men sitting on one side, and the women on the other.

5. There is the vacant lot that I was telling you about. That is where I intend to build.

6. That is mine. You know that it is. You gave it to me.

7. When my cousin returned from his hunting expedition, I did not recognize him. Because I was young when he went away.

8. The board of trustees agreed to construct an addition to the dormitory. The work to begin as soon as the weather became warm.

9. Surely you cannot say that this road is smooth. It is rough.

10. The car jolted over the uneven road. Swaying from one side to the other.

11. Frank taking the lead up the trail that wound to the top of the mountain. The little group wearily followed him.

12. Most of the residents in this community are of foreign birth. Being natives of Germany or Sweden.

13. Standing in line were many foreigners. Most of whom could not speak or understand English.

14. Here are several packages to be delivered. That one, a special order, is to be taken at once.

15. The council consisted of nine members. One of whom was the mayor.

16. In the first term we must read three books. One to be a biography and two to be novels.

17. Plodding wearily along the hot and dusty road. The two young men were tired and hungry.

18. Skating is the type of winter sport that I like best. It is less strenuous than skiing.

19. We completed the trip in three days. Driving nearly four hundred miles a day.

20. Lounging on the river bank of a little old-fashioned southern town, I became fascinated by the large, cumbersome

boats.   Which were moving so slowly that they seemed to be standing still.

21. Before the class meets, I must work three more problems. Which are unusually difficult.

22. We have two reports to write this week.   One is to be handed in Wednesday, and the other to be handed in Friday.

23. Going by way of Richmondale, which was ten miles west of Waverly.   We were able to avoid the muddy road.

24. By driving for nearly ten hours without rest.   We arrived in Chicago at the appointed time.

25. At present my roommate seems to have only one ambition. To win first place in the oratorical contest that is to be held in March.

Coordinate Clauses in Building Sentences

1. Coordinate clauses express thoughts of equal rank. Usually they are joined by a coordinate conjunction to form a compound sentence:

> The lawn is now green, and the cherry tree is full of blossoms.
> He painted the old chair, and she made a cushion for it.

2. These clauses, however, need not be joined by a conjunction. Since they are of equal rank, each is capable of standing alone as an independent sentence:

> The lawn is now green. The cherry tree is full of blossoms.
> He painted the old chair. She made a cushion for it.

Each sentence in these pairs, you see, is grammatically complete, inasmuch as each has its own subject and predicate; and neither contains a thought subordinate to that of the other. When the clauses are compounded, the coordinate conjunction — *and*, for example — belongs to neither. It merely shows that, because of a close relationship, the reader should consider the two thoughts together.

3. The reason he should do so is that the writer uses compound sentences chiefly to show comparison or contrast or to express concurrent, sequential, or alternative actions and conditions. Consider, for example, the relationship expressed in each of the following sentences:

> This poem has vivid imagery, and that one is rhythmical.
> (Comparison)

> The gardener planted the peach tree beside the garage, but he planted the cherry tree in the middle of the garden. (Contrast)
>
> Some firemen unrolled the hose, and others placed a ladder against the burning building. (Concurrent actions)
>
> The sky is black, and the air is heavy with moisture. (Concurrent conditions)
>
> The chairman sat down, and the speaker then explained the program of his organization. (Sequential actions)
>
> We must write a thousand-word paper, or we must give a twenty-minute speech. (Alternative actions)

4. In the first five of the foregoing sentences, the conjunction merely joins the two clauses; if it were omitted and each clause were written as an independent sentence, each ending with a period, the close relationship between the thoughts would still exist:

> Some firemen unrolled the hose. Others placed a ladder against the burning building.

Note, however, that *or* cannot be omitted without destroying the logical relationship.

5. A sentence may consist of more than two coordinate clauses:

> The lights in the auditorium went out, the curtain rose slowly, and the audience applauded.

From this type of sentence the conjunction is seldom omitted. It is generally used, however, only between the last two members, though it may be used between the others also.

Kinds of Coordinate Clauses

6. Coordinate clauses may be *simple* or *complex*.

7. A *simple clause* is one clause, without another clause used within it as a part of speech. When it stands alone, it

is a *simple sentence.* When two are joined, they make a *compound sentence.*

> The chairman sat down, and the speaker then explained the program of his organization.

8. A *complex clause* consists of one clause that contains another clause as a part of speech. The first is called the *main clause,* and the second is called the *dependent* or *subordinate clause.* When this kind of clause stands alone, it is known as a *complex sentence.* When it is joined by a coordinate conjunction to either a simple clause or another complex clause, the combination is called a *compound-complex sentence.* In the following sentences, the dependent clauses are italicized:

> He painted the chair *that they bought,* and she made a cushion for it.
> The chairman sat down *when he had opened the meeting,* and the speaker then gave ten reasons *why the town needed a better library.*

In sentences like these, the main clauses are coordinate, as would be clear if the dependent clauses were omitted. Without these dependent clauses, of course, the meaning would not be complete; but still they are only parts of speech in the main clauses.

9. If the coordinate conjunction is omitted from a compound-complex sentence, each of the parts is an independent sentence, which is either simple or complex.

> He painted the chair that they bought. She made a cushion for it. (The first sentence is complex; the second is simple.)
> The chairman sat down when he had opened the meeting. The speaker then gave ten reasons why the town needed a better library. (Both sentences are complex.)

10. Thus you see that the coordinate clauses of both compound and compound-complex sentences are capable

of standing alone as independent sentences. When they do stand alone, however, they are still closely related, expressing thoughts that are to be considered together. In other words, we might say that the independent sentences are so closely related in thought that they could be joined by a coordinate conjunction.

Punctuation of Coordinate Clauses

IMPROPER USE OF COMMA

11. Frequently the thought of two such sentences is so closely related that a period makes too distinct a break between them. The writer wants to show the relationship by combining the two independent clauses in a single sentence, with some mark of punctuation less heavy than a period between them. Many inexperienced writers put a comma at the end of the first clause. But a comma indicates too light a break between them when they are not connected by a coordinate conjunction; it does not sufficiently warn the reader that one grammatically independent unit has come to an end and another is about to begin. True, experienced writers occasionally use a comma in such a position, but they do so deliberately to gain certain effects. Until you are more experienced, you should not use a comma between two independent clauses not connected by a coordinate conjunction. Such objectionable usage is referred to as a *comma splice, comma fault,* or *comma blunder.*

12. To show a close relationship between structurally independent clauses not joined by a coordinate conjunction, one of two marks of punctuation is regularly used: the *semicolon* or the *colon.* These marks have other uses, but here you need to consider them only as substitutes for a period between two independent statements so closely related that they could be joined by a coordinate conjunction.

13. The semicolon is used more frequently than a colon as a substitute for a period. It indicates merely that the two statements, though independent according to structure, are closely related in thought:

> In 1564 Shakespeare was born in England. In the same year, Galileo was born in Italy.
>
> In 1564 Shakespeare was born in England; in the same year, Galileo was born in Italy.
>
> Those who are walking will leave at nine o'clock. Those who are going in cars will not leave until ten.
>
> Those who are walking will leave at nine o'clock; those who are going in cars will not leave until ten.
>
> The first row of lights will go out when you turn the top switch. The second row will go out when you turn the bottom one.
>
> The first row of lights will go out when you turn the top switch; the second row will go out when you turn the bottom one. (In sentences of this pattern, the second clause is often elliptical: *The first row of lights will go out when you turn the top switch; the second when you turn the bottom.* Here the semicolon is the only suitable mark. Since the second clause is still grammatically independent, a comma must not be used; but since it is elliptical, its meaning is so dependent upon that of the first that a period between them would be inappropriate.)

COLON SUBSTITUTED FOR PERIOD

14. A colon expresses a special type of relationship between two statements. It indicates that the second explains or amplifies the first by giving concrete details or examples. The first statement is general and the second is specific. A semicolon may be used, but the colon serves better to bring out the logical relationship.

> In 1564 a great dramatist and a pioneer scientist were
> born: these two were Shakespeare and Galileo.
> We had three options: we could read a novel, two full-
> length plays, or a volume of short stories.
> We finally decided upon a definite schedule: cars were to
> leave the main building at nine, ten, eleven, two, and
> four o'clock.

PUNCTUATION WITH A COORDINATE CONJUNCTION

15. Though a comma is inappropriate between coordinate clauses not joined by a conjunction, it is generally
used between coordinate clauses — either simple or complex — that are joined by any of the coordinate conjunctions: *and, but, or, nor.* Exceptions to this practice are
common when the clauses are very short or when commas
are needed within either one or both of the clauses.

16. Short clauses, each consisting of not more than four
or five words, are so unlikely to be misread that no mark
of punctuation is needed before the conjunction. A
comma, however, is not wrong; in fact, before *but* the
comma is often used to emphasize the contrast in thought.
Observe the following illustrations:

> The gong sounded and the curtain rose.
> The gong sounded, and the curtain rose. (You may use a
> comma, especially if you want to emphasize a pause.
> When you are in doubt, use a comma.)
> The gong sounded, but the curtain did not rise.

17. When the coordinate clauses contain commas, a
semicolon is generally used between them, preceding the
coordinate conjunction, so that the reader can readily
distinguish the members of the compound sentence from
the subordinate and independent expressions within the
members. Observe, for example, the punctuation before
the coordinate conjunctions in the following sentences.
In some of these sentences the members do not contain
commas, and so they are separated by a comma; in others

they do contain commas, and they are therefore separated by a semicolon.

> My class meets every day at ten o'clock in room 211, and his meets at eleven o'clock in room 310.
>
> I am able to take part in the track meet, but John will not be eligible until next week.
>
> The motion picture, I have been told, follows closely the plot of the book; and it faithfully reproduces the costumes of the period.
>
> When we have the picnic, the boys will bring the wood and make the fire; and the girls, according to our plan, will furnish the food. (Note that the coordinate conjunction *and* in the first clause joins two predicate verbs in the same clause, not two clauses in a compound sentence.)

18. The same principle applies to the punctuation of a series of clauses. Ordinarily these clauses, though only the last two are joined by a conjunction, are separated by commas. A comma is used between the last two clauses, preceding the conjunction, as well as between the others:

> The band played the college song, three cheerleaders in unison kept time with the music, and the students in the grandstand sang lustily.

The punctuation of this series, you see, is the same as that of any series of words or phrases:

> The old car was short, high, and bulky.
>
> The old car had high wheels, high seats, and a steering lever.

If, however, any of the clauses contains a comma, a semicolon is generally used between the clauses:

> When the team came upon the field, the band played the college song; three cheerleaders, each in a costume of different color, kept time with the music; and the students in the grandstand, all waving the college colors, sang lustily.

19. Note that after each member of a series, including the one preceding the conjunction, the same mark of punctuation is used, whether it be a comma or a semicolon.

Summary

20. The purposes of the discussion in this Study Unit are two. The first one is to tell you how coordinate clauses are constructed and how you may use them in building sentences; the second, equally important, is primarily to show how coordinate clauses are punctuated when a period obscures the closeness of the relationship between them and when they are not joined by a coordinate conjunction. Since these clauses are grammatically independent, even though they are closely related in thought, you should *not* separate them with a comma. You should use a semicolon or, in certain situations, a colon.

EXERCISE 42. Coordinate Clauses with and without Connectives

State the kind of punctuation mark that should be used to separate the coordinate clauses in each of the following sentences. Note that some of the coordinate clauses are joined by conjunctions and some are not.

1. On one side of the small lake was a boathouse on the other side was a pier for swimmers.
2. The band was playing the favorite college song and the students were singing lustily though most of them obviously did not know the words.
3. Your skates are new and sharp mine have been in storage so long that they are rusty.
4. We left for camp early in the morning the others followed as soon as their car arrived.
5. The play was better than any that we had given previously but the audience did not like it.

6. One attendant put air into the tires another washed the windshield.
7. When we closed the window the room was too hot for us to stay awake when we opened it the wind blew all of the papers off our desks.
8. When the lights in the auditorium gradually became dim the orchestra played softly and the curtain slowly opened for the first act of a lurid melodrama that was full of complicated intrigues and thrilling escapes.
9. The first speaker explained the purpose of the constitutional amendment the second one urged us to vote for it.
10. The federal government may make laws governing interstate commerce the state can make laws that govern only intrastate commerce.

EXERCISE 43. Coordinate Clauses with and without Connectives

Identify each complete sentence in the following exercise — whether it be simple, compound, complex, or compound-complex — by stating exactly where it begins and where it ends. Then state the kind of punctuation mark that should be used between the coordinate clauses.

One summer a classmate of mine joined me in an enterprise that we thought would be profitable it was nothing original or even unusual Jerry and I knew that many college students had undertaken it in preceding years what we did not know was that only a few had succeeded our "enterprise" was simply that of selling a one-volume encyclopedia a bright red book containing general information about subjects of common interest everybody wanted it the publishers said and most people would buy it we should have known better but we did not with enthusiasm we set out to make our fortune or at least enough of it to pay our college expenses with experience we came back disillusioned the public we discovered was not so eager for knowledge as we had supposed our big mistake perhaps was in going to the wrong territory the company offered us a limited choice of what it called "sales territories" and without knowing much about any of them we blindly selected a rugged hilly region that included a few sleepy towns and much unproductive farm land the people we soon discovered were impoverished and were indifferent to the opportunity we offered them their response was generally the same everywhere they had no money they did not want the book

Our handicap no doubt was that we were not good salesmen Jerry admitted that he was not but because of some earlier success I thought I could sell anything the result was that we decided to divide the work I was to sell the books Jerry was to deliver them and collect the money he was excellent at that kind of work but unfortunately he had little opportunity to show what he could do the obvious reason was that I could not sell the books I sold a few every day but not enough to pay our expenses we continued to work hard but every day our hope faded at the end of the first week we were discouraged at the end of the second we were frightened on Saturday we paid our bills and counted the money we had left it was less than we had when we arrived Jerry urged that we leave at once and go home he was sensible I was not I wanted to prove to ourselves that we could succeed I was standing at the window of our dingy room trying to think of how we could sell more books Jerry sat at a little table still looking at our balance sheet suddenly both of us realized that we had only two dollars more than the price of two railroad tickets and at once we began to pack

Coordinate Clauses: Special Problems

1. You need to be particularly on your guard against committing a comma error — that is, using a comma to separate two coordinate clauses not connected by a conjunction — in two constructions: (a) when the second clause is introduced by a conjunctive adverb; (b) when the second clause begins with a pronoun.

Clauses Introduced by Conjunctive Adverbs

2. In a pair of coordinate clauses the second is often introduced by an independent element that indicates the logical relationship between the two. Such a word or group of words is sometimes called a conjunctive adverb, and although that name is not entirely satisfactory it will be used in the discussion that follows. A conjunctive adverb may indicate that the second thought is in addition to the first (*likewise, besides, moreover, furthermore, also, too*), in contrast to it (*however, nevertheless, yet, on the other hand, on the contrary*), in consequence of it (*therefore, so, thus, accordingly, hence, for this reason*), or explanatory of it (*for example, for instance, that is, in other words*).

> The weather this winter has been unusually warm. *Moreover*, there has been very little rain and snow.
> All of us warned him against the danger of climbing the mountain. He, *however*, was convinced that he would be safe.

191

> The weather this winter has been unusually warm.   The
> buds on the trees, *therefore*, have appeared too early.
> We are working under several difficulties.   *For example*,
> the office space is entirely inadequate.

You observe that such words may appear at the beginning
of the second sentence or in some later position.

PUNCTUATION WITH CONJUNCTIVE ADVERBS

3. You can see that the thoughts of two such sentences
may be so closely related that a period marks too distinct
a separation between them.   Often it is preferable to
combine them into a single sentence.   If you do so, however, you must remember the rule you learned in the preceding Study Unit.   Separate the two clauses by means of
a semicolon or in some cases (See paragraphs 9–11 below)
a colon.   *Do not separate them by means of a comma.*

4. You are not likely to do so when the conjunctive adverb comes after the beginning of the second sentence, as in
the second and third examples above.   If you are not on
your guard, however, you might make this mistake when
the conjunctive adverb comes at the head of its sentence,
as it sometimes does.   In this position it often shows more
emphatically the close relationship between the thoughts,
as you can see in the following reconstructions of two of
the foregoing examples:

> All of us warned him against the danger of climbing the
> mountain; however, he was convinced that he would
> be safe.
> The weather this winter has been unusually warm; there-
> fore the buds on the trees have appeared too early.

At the head of the sentence, the conjunctive function of
the adverb is more conspicuous, and so you might be mis-
led into calling it a conjunction, which may be preceded
by a comma.   Remember that, regardless of its position,
it is not a conjunction, and so it does not in itself warrant
the use of a comma between the sentences.

5. A conjunctive adverb at the head of a clause does not *in itself* warrant the use of a comma at the end of the preceding clause; but a comma *may* be used *if the two clauses are joined by a coordinate conjunction*, as in the following sentences:

> We completed our work, and so we wrote the final report.
> Our friend told us clearly how to drive out of the city, and consequently he saved us from the ordeal of seeking our way.
> The mountains were nearly a hundred miles away, but still I could see their snowcapped peaks.
> Our expenses in giving this play will be high, and therefore we must sell an unusually large number of tickets if we are to make a profit.

These, of course, are merely compound sentences whose members are joined by coordinate conjunctions; and so their punctuation should be governed by the same principle as has already been given for sentences of this type. If the members do not contain commas, they should be separated by commas; if they do contain commas, they should be separated by semicolons.

SOME TROUBLESOME CONSTRUCTIONS

6. *So.* There is an increasing tendency to punctuate *so* as if it were a coordinate conjunction.

> I have not read the book, so I cannot recommend it.

The most careful writers, however, consider *so* a conjunctive adverb, to be preceded by a semicolon unless it is combined with *and*.

> I have not read the book; so I cannot recommend it.
> I have not read the book, and so I cannot recommend it.

7. *So that.* The subordinate connective *so that* sometimes misleads inexperienced writers, because they see only the *so* at the head of a clause, call it a conjunctive

adverb, and then put a semicolon in front of it. Actually, of course, the two words form a compound connective which is always used to introduce a dependent clause. Since a dependent clause cannot stand alone as a sentence, it is never separated from the main clause by a semicolon:

> We arranged our work so that we could attend the dance.
> The magazines were placed on a rack in the main reading room so that they would be readily accessible.

8. *However.* The word *however* is also confusing. Usually it is a conjunctive adverb, but sometimes it stands at the head of a subordinate clause of concession. Consider the following sentences:

> I could not get the correct answer to the problem; however, I shall try again tomorrow. (Here *however* is a conjunctive adverb.)
> I could not get the correct answer to the problem, however hard I tried. (Here *however* introduces a subordinate clause, which of course should not be set apart from the main clause by a semicolon. This becomes clearer if the position of the two clauses is reversed.)
> I could not get the correct answer to the problem. However hard I tried, I always made a mistake. (Here the subordinate clause goes with the second main clause; hence if the two sentences were combined into one, a semicolon before *however* would be proper.)

THE COLON WITH CONJUNCTIVE ADVERBS

9. In the preceding Study Unit you learned that when two independent statements are combined in a single sentence, they may be separated by a colon instead of a semicolon when the first makes a general statement and the second gives a definite illustration or explanation of it. In such a situation the second clause is frequently introduced by such a conjunctive adverb as *for example, for instance, that is, in other words.* Hence these expressions,

when they introduce a clause, are often preceded by a colon, although a semicolon may also be used.

> Here are several novels about spectacular periods in our history. For example, these two recount the struggles and privations of the California pioneers in 1859. (The period after *history* may be replaced by a semicolon or, preferably, a colon.)
>
> This entry violates the first rule of the contest. That is, it exceeds five thousand words in length. (Here again a colon or a semicolon might replace the period after *contest.*)

10. In sentences of this type, in which a particularly close relationship between the two statements is expressed, you may need to be especially on your guard against using a comma between the two clauses. If you need help in seeing the grammatical completeness of each of the clauses, try omitting the introductory words:

> Here are several novels about spectacular periods in our history. These two recount the struggles and privations of the California pioneers in 1859.
>
> This entry violates the first rule of the contest. It exceeds five thousand words in length.

In each group, each sentence is obviously able to stand alone. If the members of a pair are combined in a single sentence, they must be separated by a semicolon or a colon, never by a comma. Remember that the insertion of *for example* or *that is* has no effect upon this basic punctuation.

11. CAUTION. Note carefully, however, that when such an introductory phrase introduces a group of words that do *not* form a clause capable of standing alone, either a comma or a colon may precede the introductory phrase.

> We were allowed to take only two pieces of baggage, for example, a small steamer trunk and a suitcase.
>
> I ask only one thing: that is, a quiet place to work.

You see, of course, that the words following the introductory phrase form an appositive.

Clauses Introduced by Pronouns

12. The second construction in which you are particularly likely to commit the comma error is that in which the second of two coordinate clauses not connected by a conjunction begins with a personal, indefinite, or demonstrative pronoun. Consider the following pairs of thoughts:

> Tomorrow my little brother is to take his first train ride; *he* is so excited that he can hardly eat.
> The eleven members of the team function like parts in a complicated machine; *each* knows what he is to do in every play, and he performs according to instructions.
> If you want to go to Lebanon, you are on the wrong road; *this* goes to Lafayette.

Inexperienced writers often separate such statements by means of a comma, or use no punctuation at all between them. They assume mistakenly that since the meaning of the pronoun is not clear without its antecedent, which is in the preceding clause, the two clauses belong together; but, as is pointed out in Study Unit 6, although a pronoun may not be logically complete without its antecedent, it is grammatically capable of standing as the subject of a sentence. Such pairs of thoughts as the preceding ones therefore follow the principles of punctuation laid down in the preceding Study Unit. The fact that the second clause has a pronoun rather than a noun as subject does not alter the situation.

13. Frequently such pairs of thoughts are distinct enough to warrant writing each as an independent sentence. Sometimes the relationship between them is better expressed by a semicolon or colon. The following pairs of statements are correctly separated, but between some of them any one of the three marks — period, semicolon. or colon — might be used in order to represent

accurately the degree and kind of relationship intended by the writer. What you need to keep in mind is that both parts are grammatically complete and independent, so that a comma cannot be used between them.

> These sweaters will be awarded to members of our football team. They are the best that we could buy.
>
> These sweaters will be awarded to members of our football team; they are the best that we could buy.
>
> Over there is our new car. It is the first that we have owned.
>
> Over there is our new car; it is the first that we have owned.
>
> The children of the second grade marched upon the stage to sing Christmas carols. Each wore a red cape and carried a song book.
>
> The children of the second grade marched upon the stage to sing Christmas carols; each wore a red cape and carried a song book.
>
> Here are several books for you to read. This is the most interesting.
>
> Here are several books for you to read; this is the most interesting.
>
> I have my pencil. That must be yours.
>
> I have my pencil; that must be yours.
>
> The eleven members of the football team function like a complicated machine. Each knows what he is to do in every play, and he performs according to instructions.
>
> The eleven members of the football team function like a complicated machine: each knows what he is to do in every play, and he performs according to instructions.

EXERCISE 44.   Clauses Introduced
by Conjunctive Adverbs

Supply internal punctuation for the following groups of words:

1. Both the director and the actors thought the play was excellent however the audience did not like it.
2. We drove until noon then we had dinner and rested an hour before we continued our journey.
3. This summer has been unusually hot in fact it is perhaps the hottest we have had in the last ten years.
4. Most of the long building was only three stories high in the center however was a five-story tower.
5. If you cannot find your skates you may use mine furthermore you may wear my new wool cap.
6. In the winter we are fortunate in having a variety of outdoor sports for instance we can skate at the municipal rink or we can ski in the high mountains.
7. You come upon the stage through the right door then you walk to the table and look back.
8. The wind was blowing so much snow against our windshield that we could scarcely see nevertheless we drove slowly and cautiously to the next town.
9. Each page of the calendar showed three months that is it showed the current month in large type with the preceding and succeeding months below it in smaller type.
10. The stage was so dimly illuminated with green and blue lights that we could not tell one character from another in fact we did not know at first that the actors were on the stage we could not distinguish them from the furniture.
11. Before we went on our fishing trip each member of the group accepted definite responsibilities for making and maintaining our camp thus everyone knew from the outset how much work he must do.
12. When the curtain first opened we could not see the stage then our eyes became accustomed to the dim light and we

gradually identified two persons in long flowing robes moving about like ghosts.
13. You ought to make a conscientious effort to enlarge your vocabulary for example you ought to try to add one new word each day.
14. You should make a conscientious effort to increase your vocabulary otherwise you will not be able to express yourself adequately.
15. You must know more about a word than its meaning that is you must know how to spell and pronounce it.

EXERCISE 45. Clauses Introduced by Conjunctive Adverbs

In the following paragraphs state what marks of punctuation would be appropriate at the end of sentences and between coordinate clauses.

A. Though Shakespeare is generally recognized as the greatest English poet we have only a little exact knowledge of his life many scholars however have pieced together the fragments of information and by correlating these with other known facts of the period they have been able to fill in some of the gaps for example we do not know the day of the month when Shakespeare was born but we have a dated record of his baptism which occurred on April 26, 1564 moreover we know that infants were customarily baptized within a few days after their birth consequently we can be reasonably certain that he was born sometime in April 1564 additional evidence is provided by the monument over his grave in Stratford-on-Avon which tells us that when he died on April 23, 1616 he was fifty-three years of age thus we can come to the one positive conclusion that he was born before April 24 this kind of evidence obviously leads to nothing specific but it does narrow the range of possibilities the dates of other events in his early life are equally uncertain we still do not know exactly when he married Anne Hathaway and we have no information that would warrant even a guess nevertheless we do know that a license for the two of them to wed was issued November 27, 1582 likewise we do not know when his children were born the Parish Registers of Stratford however record the baptism of Susanna on May 26, 1583 then they record the baptism of their twins Hamnet and Judith nearly two years later on February 2, 1585 after this date we have a long gap of seven years in which Shakespeare is nowhere mentioned then in 1592 we discover that he is in London we do not know when he went there furthermore we have no definite information about what he did in the interval we know only that he was already successful enough to be noticed by some of the older playwrights

B. Easier means of travel and communication in this country have resulted in what some people regard as a cultural loss that is they have tended to modify the characteristics that made one locality different from others a few areas have retained their individualities but many have so completely lost theirs that they are exactly like their neighbors this merging of characteristics is most noticeable in the central Mississippi Valley where people have been unusually mobile and have also been in the path of travel between the East and the West for example one can now drive from Pittsburgh to Omaha without being aware of any striking differences among the people a hundred years ago one could not cross Ohio and Indiana without noticing that communities had personalities in fact one might sometimes have felt the strangeness of being in a foreign country even the language though recognizable as English was spoken differently this distinctiveness came from an interaction between nature and people that is the environment had certain qualities that affected the people and the people had peculiarities that colored their environment and their community life for this reason these localities were called "local color" areas though they are gradually disappearing they have been preserved in literature numerous short stories for instance give us sharply focused views of the various aspects of an area such as those pertaining to environment religious practice moral taboos social customs and personal idiosyncrasies for example Mary E. Wilkins Freeman wrote about New England O. Henry about New York City Thomas Nelson Page about Virginia Hamlin Garland about the wheat belt and Bret Harte about California of the gold rush days the titles of some of their stories are well known most people for instance have at least heard of "A New England Nun" "The Gift of the Magi" "Marse Chan" "Among the Corn Rows" and "The Luck of Roaring Camp" many stories of this type unfortunately have little merit as literature in fact some are less than mediocre but most of them provide us with a vivid record of how our people once lived

Exercise 46.   Clauses Beginning
with a Pronoun

Supply internal punctuation for the following groups of words:

1. Your order for tickets came last week this came yesterday in the afternoon mail.
2. My secretary wrote him last week acknowledging the receipt of his order he should have received the letter yesterday.
3. In the hangar are two new airplanes which arrived only yesterday each is now being equipped as a laboratory in order to test aeronautical instruments at high altitudes.
4. When the box office opens tomorrow morning you will still be able to reserve good seats none of those in the first two rows of the balcony which are excellent have been sold.
5. The seats provided for the meeting were in orderly rows but they consisted of everything available some were rickety chairs and others were rude benches that bristled with splinters nearly everyone in the audience preferred to stand.
6. When I entered the room I felt dizzy all of the numerous pictures on the walls were hanging crooked.

7. Last Saturday night when we drove into the town a small midwestern community we found cars parked side by side at the curbs and people crowding the streets they had come for miles we were told in order to do their weekly shopping.

8. The instructor pointed to the number at the bottom of the page that little figure he told us was the correct answer to the problem.

9. The machines along the north wall are lathes those on the other side of the room are drill presses.

10. Jerry stood in line for hours waiting for the gate to open he was so eager to see a world series' game that he would have been willing to stand all night in order to get a ticket.

EXERCISE 47. Clauses Beginning with a Pronoun

In the following exercise state which marks of punctuation would be appropriate at the end of sentences and between coordinate clauses.

Circuses were made for boys others go to see them and they no doubt enjoy them but boys live them they are too young to realize the hardships and hazards involved in moving constantly and in giving performances twice a day in all kinds of weather they see only the excitement and the glamour some dream of themselves as swinging dangerously on a high trapeze riding sleek horses bareback or bobbing up and down on the head of an elephant others see visions of themselves as ringmasters those magnificent men in tall hats and cutaway coats who are constantly snapping long sinewy whips the greatest ambition of every boy of course is to be a clown but no youngster if he had a real opportunity would refuse a job even as roustabout that to be sure would require hard work but hardship is pleasure when it takes one into the land of enchantment one may then live only in the borderland of magic but still he is under its spell

Probably conditions have changed so much that boys no longer dream of circuses there are now only a few of them touring the country fifty years ago more than a dozen well-known circuses crisscrossed the country several were as large as today's biggest show a few were small but all of them were good everyone who was a boy in those years remembers their names the period was roughly from 1890 to 1914 that was the Golden Age for boys those who lived in the smaller communities probably had the most fun they got up early to see the train arrive they watched the unloading of the wagons the horses the camels and the elephants when the horses were hitched to wagons many of which contained animals from all parts of the world they followed the procession to the circus grounds some of them got jobs that would assure them free tickets to the show others followed the parade uptown and then if they were lucky enough to wangle fifty cents from their parents they went in ecstasy to the afternoon performance

EXERCISE 48.   Sentence Recognition

In the following exercise state which marks of punctuation would be appropriate at the end of sentences and between coordinate clauses.

Although floods along a big river generally rise slowly enough for all inhabitants to leave the danger zone I recall one that rushed with torrential suddenness upon Chesterfield this town which had been built in the angle that was formed by the juncture of the Ohio and one of her wide sluggish tributaries was constantly threatened the water covered some part of the town every spring and several times it had flooded the chief business section in all of these floods however the rivers had risen not more than a foot a day so that the residents could be warned of coming danger numerous reports from towns up the river furthermore had always helped them anticipate probable conditions in their own community as an additional precaution they recently had built a flood wall which they said would keep out sixty-two feet of water consequently they now felt especially safe this feeling of security was fortified too by the records of high-water stages which showed that the river seldom had risen above the nine-foot stage for the foregoing reasons they ought to have felt well protected against any ordinary flood what they could not foresee though was that this one was not to be ordinary its beginning was similar to that of all others but not its ending at first a warm spring rain which lasted nearly a week melted the snow and ice in all of the territory that drained into the two rivers after several days of this drainage along their courses they naturally began to rise all of the people thought however that as soon as the snow and ice had been melted the rivers would recede without doing any damage the second week though brought a series of thunderstorms that dropped sheets of water for miles around then the people became excited frantically they built boats moved household goods and merchandise to second floors and boarded up expensive plate-glass windows to many skeptical people these preparations seemed premature however they were nothing short of providential because early one morning warning came that a large dam at the headwaters of the tributary had broken two hours later a wall of water rushed down the valley and flooded the whole town except a few high places when dawn came the downtown streets looked like those seen in pictures of Venice many people in boats some of them crude homemade ones were rowing through the streets most of these people of course were on serious business such as that of moving valuable goods rescuing marooned persons and carrying supplies however a large number of them seemed to be out merely for the novelty of riding through the streets in boats they were having a rollicking good time as if a magnificent water carnival were being staged for their special benefit perhaps they were unusually light-hearted and unaware of the loss and suffering that this catastrophe was bringing on the other hand perhaps they already had lost everything but their lives and now were jesting hysterically with fate

EXERCISE 49.   Sentence Recognition

In the following exercise state which marks of punctuation would be appropriate at the end of sentences and between coordinate clauses.

Charles Dickens who is one of the best-known English novelists was born February 7 1812 into an environment that gave no promise of his later fame though his father John Dickens had a fair income from his position as a clerk in the Navy Pay Office the family always was poor the father in fact was so frequently unable to pay his debts that he often was in prison he was not too lazy to work but he seldom had enough money to meet his expenses what the exact reason was we do not know Charles Dickens tells us that his father was industrious kind and generous moreover he was always optimistic two of these splendid qualities of course might have been the cause of his poverty that is he may have been so generous and optimistic that his friends took unfair advantage of him another probable cause however was his constantly increasing family a family that later included eight children we of course are less interested in the causes of this poverty than in the results one of the most important being the irregular schooling that the children received being the oldest boy in this thriftless impoverished debt-ridden family Charles was obliged to begin work when he was still a child consequently his formal education was limited to two short periods in day schools one of these periods being in an ordinary school in London

His first job which he was obliged to take at the age of about ten years was in a warehouse here his surroundings were sordid and depressing and most of his fellow workers in this dingy environment were crude the result was that he toiled through several humiliating and unhappy years at the age of fifteen he was employed in a lawyer's office which the English call a "solicitor's" office apparently he did not like this work for he remained in it only a year or two the exact length of this period is unknown the record shows however that in 1829 approximately two years after he entered the solicitor's office he became a reporter on one of the London newspapers with this change he set the course of his future he must have known that he had found his life's work for he immediately began to put in much of his leisure time reading in the British Museum thus he no doubt hoped to gain at least a part of the education missed in school furthermore he became proficient in using shorthand having studied diligently in his spare moments so that when he listened to speeches he could take notes rapidly

Nearly as soon as he commenced his newpaper work and his program of diligent reading he began to write stories December 1833 is the date of the publication of the first of these a short story that was called *A Dinner at Poplar Walk* not many people however know that Dickens wrote it a few of his admirers have read it others have not even heard of it three years later, in 1836, *Sketches by Boz* was published in two volumes all of the stories in these books however had already been published in the *Monthly Magazine* they are now considered important for only one reason they show that he had talent in the year following the publication of *Sketches by Boz* that is in 1837 Dickens published the book that gave him wide popularity this was his well-known *Pickwick Papers* then appeared in rapid succession a number of well-known novels namely *Oliver Twist, Nicholas Nickleby, Old Curiosity Shop, Barnaby Rudge,* and *Martin Chuzzlewit* these novels all of them long he published between 1838 and 1844 that is he wrote five important novels within a short period of six years this achievement would have been enough for most people however Dickens crowded into these few years many other strenuous endeavors for example he made a four-months' trip to the United States where he gave numerous lectures wrote his *American Notes* which recorded his observations in the United States and brought out a short story that has been popular with every succeeding generation the *Christmas Carol* these publications were followed by many others the most popular being *David Copperfield* this was a favorite not only with Dickens' readers but also with Dickens himself his last novel was *The Mystery of Edwin Drood* which was still unfinished when the author died

June 9 1870 marks the end of his brilliant colorful career his whole life being short the years that he was able to give to writing were limited by his early death nevertheless within the hurried crowded span of thirty-two years counting from the publication of *Oliver Twist* we find that he wrote fifteen novels and many other books beginning life as an impoverished uneducated inconspicuous child as one among thousands he rose by tireless feverish energy to international fame

Exercise 50. Sentence Recognition

In the following exercise state which marks of punctuation would be appropriate at the end of sentences and between coordinate clauses.

Galileo lived in an age when experimental science was not popular that is new scientific conclusions were not proved by means of experiments though laboratories are common to us they were unknown in his day science of course was taught in the universities but it was entirely different from what we call science it was according to our definition not science at all because it did not contain a body of facts that could be verified by experience moreover it was not based upon inductive reasoning as ours is it was based upon deductive reasoning the learned men of those times in other words derived their conclusions by reasoning from laws that had been handed down from authorities the chief of them being Aristotle a Greek philosopher the conclusions that he had stated centuries before were looked upon as basic infallible laws and to doubt them was heresy for this reason when Galileo who was a professor of mathematics in the University of Pisa Italy tried to prove to his colleagues that some of these so-called scientific axioms were wrong he was ridiculed and was even persecuted

Those of us who perform experiments almost every day in our laboratory classes can hardly imagine this condition it existed however only a little more than three hundred years ago which is not a long period in the history of mankind Galileo we must remember was born February 15 1564 in Pisa Italy near Florence in the same year Shakespeare was born in England and only fifty-six years later the Pilgrims landed at Plymouth on the rocky and uninviting coast of a country that was to contribute to the development of science as much as has any other country in the world in those early days however Tycho Brahe, John Kepler, and Galileo were actually risking their lives to prove some of the facts that we now consider as fundamental to astronomy, mathematics, and mechanics

The account of an experiment performed by Galileo for instance illustrates how these men the enthusiastic undaunted and restless pioneers of modern science struggled and suffered to convince not only their fellow workers the scientists and mathematicians of their day but also the people of the world Galileo was convinced that Aristotle's law of falling bodies which was accepted by his colleagues was wrong this law which was believed by all learned men the philosophers of his time was that two falling objects of unequal weight would drop at a speed proportional to their weight or in other words that the heavier object would strike the ground first these objects of course were to be of the same material though this belief never before had been questioned Galileo dared to say that it was unreasonable for an object twice as large as another would then be upon the ground at the time that the other was still in mid-air his theory was that both would strike the ground at the same time his colleagues scoffed at the idea but he stubbornly held to his own theory moreover he arranged to demonstrate that he was right he took two objects of unequal weight to the top of the Leaning Tower of Pisa which was in the same city where the University was located his colleagues having assembled at the base of the tower he dropped both objects at the same time both of them as Galileo had predicted struck the ground simultaneously his colleagues saw what had happened but they were not convinced they maintained in spite of the evidence that the demonstration was unsound for Aristotle their accepted authority had said that the heavier object must strike the ground first so obstinate were they that they ridiculed Galileo brought charges of insubordination against him and forced him to give up his position in the University today however we know that he was right his conclusion has often been verified by our experimentation in fact it is now looked upon as one of the fundamental laws of dynamics

Section C
Special Problems within the Structure

Agreement

1. When you construct a sentence, you are likely to be perplexed by some problems in agreement and case. The purpose of Section C is not to discuss these topics fully, because you undoubtedly know much about them already, but to clarify those usages that are likely to puzzle you when you construct sentences. This Study Unit treats only *agreement*.

2. The rules governing agreement concern only two kinds of words. A verb must agree with its subject, and a pronoun must agree with its antecedent.

Agreement of Verb with Subject

3. A verb must agree with its subject in person and number. As was pointed out in Study Unit 5, paragraph 14, the agreement of a verb with its subject is simple in modern English, since there are special forms to indicate person and number only in the third person singular present indicative and in the various forms of the verb *to be*. Nevertheless, there are a few perplexing problems that arise in making the verb agree in *number*.

SPECIAL PROBLEMS IN AGREEMENT

4. When a noun of different number from that of the subject comes between the subject and the verb, the verb still agrees with the subject. You must guard carefully against a natural tendency to make the verb agree with the nearer noun, especially when the verb is far removed

from its subject by intervening words, phrases, or clauses and when the subject is *kind, type,* or *sort.*

> The houses that were continually being bathed in the smoke from the foundry *were* dirty.
>
> The hands of my watch *are* loose.
>
> The age of those large cedar trees *has* not *been determined.*
>
> The purr of these motors *indicates* that they are in good order.
>
> The height of those two towers *makes* the building seem squat.
>
> A classification of the books by titles *helps* one to find the books readily.
>
> The same type of plays *was used* in every game.
>
> The kind of plates that you need to match your set *has been sold.*
>
> This sort of oranges *has* no seeds.
>
> This kind of strawberries *is* the sweetest.

Note that in sentences like the last two the demonstrative adjective *this* or *that* must agree with the subject and not with the object in the prepositional phrase.

> WRONG: These (those) kind of strawberries is sweetest.
> RIGHT: This (that) kind of strawberries is sweetest.

5. This kind of construction often gives trouble when the subject is a singular indefinite pronoun.

> Each of these boys *is* well qualified for the position.
> Either of those books *is* a good choice for a gift.
> Neither of the possibilities *attracts* me.

Some writers consider *none* invariably singular, but in modern usage it is more commonly considered either singular or plural, according to the sentence in which it occurs.

> None of the boys *are* here.
> None of the work *has* been finished.

6. When words and phrases introduced by *including, with, together with, in addition to, as well as, no less than,*

and not, or *but not* come between the subject and verb, the verb still agrees with the subject. These intervening expressions are similar to parenthetical additions to the sentence; therefore they are not a part of the subject and do not influence the number of the verb. The following sentences illustrate correct usage:

> Our camping *equipment*, including a fishing rod and two guns, *was lost* in the fire.
>
> This *steak* with mushrooms *tastes* good.
>
> *Uncle John*, together with his wife and children, *has gone* to Buffalo.
>
> This leather *jacket* in addition to your flannel shirt and heavy sweater *is* enough to keep you warm.
>
> *Fred*, as well as his brother, *is* a good student.
>
> *Fred*, no less than his brother, *is* a good student.
>
> The *door*, and not the windows, *was* open.
>
> The *chairs*, but not the table, *are* to be moved.

Sentences like the last two, which generally are awkward, can be better expressed as follows:

> The door was open, and not the windows.
>
> The chairs are to be moved, but not the table.

7. When a verb is followed by a predicate noun of different number from that of the subject, the verb still agrees with the subject.

> The daily production of this factory alone *was* ten thousand pairs of shoes.
>
> The signal for starting the train *was* three blasts of the whistle.

8. When the subject follows the verb, the verb still agrees with the subject. This inverted construction is especially likely to mislead you if a noun that is not the subject precedes the verb or if the clause begins with the expletive *there*. In the following sentences the subject is in boldface, and the verb is italicized.

In the boat *were* four **men.**

Asleep on the hard metal bench *were* two young **children.**

In front of the house there *are* three **trees.**

If you need more, there *are* some **pencils** on my desk.

9. A compound subject composed of two or more subjects joined by *and* requires a plural verb. Each of the subjects may be either singular or plural.

My brother and sister *were* here.

My brothers and sister *were* here.

My brother and sisters *were* here.

Three straight chairs, a rocker, a bookcase, two small tables, and a large study table *were* in the room.

A piece of chalk and an eraser *were* on the floor.

10. Two or more singular subjects connected by *or, either . . . or,* or *neither . . . nor* require a singular verb. Two or more plural subjects in such a construction require a plural verb.

John or Fred *was* captain of the team last year.

Either John or Fred *is* captain now.

Was John or Fred the captain of last year's team?

Neither Tom nor Bob *was* captain.

Neither the pencils nor the blotters *are* on the table.

Either the windows or the doors *are* open.

When the subjects in such a construction are of different numbers, the verb must agree with the nearer or nearest subject.

Those little boys or their dog *has taken* the ball.

Have those boys or their dog *taken* the ball?

Either the chairs or the table *has been* moved.

Neither the door nor the windows *were* ever open.

Neither the chalk, the pencils, nor the book *was* on the shelf.

This usage applies also when the subject consists of two or more pronouns that individually require different forms of a verb.

Either you or he *is going* to the library.
Neither she nor I *am going.*

When pronouns like these must be used, however, a smoother statement is as follows:

Either you are going to the library or he is.
She is not going nor am I.

11. A collective noun — that is, a noun naming a group of individuals by means of a singular form, such as *group*, *audience*, *crowd*, *class*, or *committee* — requires a plural verb when the action or condition is that of individuals within the group, and a singular verb when the action or condition is that of the group as a unit. Often this distinction in meaning is difficult, even for the writer of the sentence; whenever it is, it probably is unimportant.

When I left, the committee *were* still *arguing* about the date for the dance. (The individuals were still arguing with one another.)

The committee *has* a report to present to the class. (The committee as a unit has agreed upon a report.)

The senior class *are inviting* their friends in the junior and sophomore classes to their dance. (Individual members are inviting guests.)

The senior class *has announced* the date for its dance. (The class as a unit has announced the date.)

12. Certain nouns that are plural in form but singular in meaning, such as *politics*, *economics*, *physics*, and *mathematics*, require a singular verb. *Athletics* may be construed as either singular or plural.

Politics *is* a subject in which every student should be interested.

Mathematics *includes* arithmetic and geometry.

Suitable athletics for all students *is* (or *are*) important in the program of every school.

This usage is followed also with subjects like those in the following sentences, in which the subject is considered as a unit.

> Fifty dollars *was offered* as a reward.
> Two times four *is* eight.
> A hundred pounds of cement *is used* in the mixture.
> Five years *is* the term of his appointment.

13. The verb in a relative clause agrees with the subject of the clause; since the subject is a relative pronoun that stands for an antecedent, the verb must express the same number as the antecedent.

> It is you who *are* causing the delay.
> It is I who *am* coming, not she.

Agreement in this type of sentence is especially perplexing when the relative is preceded by a construction beginning with *one of*.

> My brother has read one of the books that *are* named on this list. (That *books*, not *one*, is the antecedent of *that* may be seen by a rearrangement of the sentence: "Of the books that are named on this list, my brother has read one." Hence the verb of the relative clause must be plural.)
> One of the books that *are* named on this list *is* missing from the library. (The verb of the relative clause is plural, agreeing with *that*, which is plural because *books*, its antecedent, is plural; but the verb of the main clause is singular, agreeing with its subject *one*.)
> One of the best novels that *have* been published this year is now in the library.
> One of the most difficult problems that *have* been given to any class was solved by the newest student.
> One of the best musicians who *have* ever been in this city is to play at the Lyric Theater tonight. (In each of the last four sentences the relative pronoun refers to the

plural noun that is the object of the preposition *of;* hence the verb in the relative clause must be in the plural.)

14. A common error is the use of *don't* for *doesn't* when a third person singular verb is required. Remember that *don't* is the contraction of *do not, doesn't* of *does not.* The following sentences are correct:

> Mr. White's name doesn't appear on the program.
> He doesn't speak today.
> Walter doesn't see us.
> She doesn't want to go.
> It doesn't count.

Agreement of Pronoun with Antecedent

15. A pronoun must agree with its antecedent in person, gender, and number. It need not agree with its antecedent in case.

16. Agreement in person is so obvious that you are not likely to have any trouble with it; but agreement in gender and number may present some perplexities.

AGREEMENT IN GENDER

17. Pronouns referring to singular nouns of common gender, such as *student, juror, member,* and *delegate,* modified by adjectives like *each, every,* and *any* are regularly masculine:

> Every member of the club has paid *his* dues. (But note as an exception such a sentence as "Every member of the Women's Guild has paid her dues.")
> Each juror, in turn, raised *his* right hand to take oath.
> Every member of the class cast *his* ballot for one candidate.
> Any delegate may be absent from the meeting if *he* has a good excuse.

This usage applies also to pronouns that have as antecedents indefinite pronouns like *everyone*, *everybody*, *anyone*, and *anybody:*

> Everyone was in *his* seat when the bell rang.
> Anybody may leave as soon as *he* has finished *his* work.

An exception is the statement that intends for emphasis to distinguish the sexes:

> Each man and woman signed *his* and *her* name to the petition.

18. Of the relative pronouns, *who* (*whom*) is masculine or feminine, *which* and *what* are neuter, and *that* is any of the three genders:

> The girl *who* won the essay contest is my cousin.
> This brief case belongs to the man *whom* you met yesterday.
> This scarf, *which* my father gave me for Christmas, is very warm.
> The book *that* I read last night was exciting.
> There is the horse *that* won the race.
> The man *that* I just spoke to is an old friend of mine.

AGREEMENT IN NUMBER

19. When a pronoun refers to a word like *everyone*, *everybody*, *every*, *each*, *any*, *either*, and *neither* or to a noun modified by one of them, the pronoun must be singular, inasmuch as each of these words is singular:

> Everyone has arranged to bring *his* lunch to the picnic.
> Every book is in *its* place.
> Each boy was carrying *his* canteen.
> Each was carrying *his* canteen.
> Any of the boys is willing to drive *his* car in the parade.
> Either boy is willing to give *his* share.
> Either is willing to give *his* share.
> Neither of the girls has brought *her* music.

The teacher will call on anyone who puts up *his* hand.
(*His* refers to *who*, which is singular because it stands
for *anyone*.)

20. When a pronoun refers to a collective noun, such as
class, *committee*, *faculty*, and *council*, it is singular if the
meaning of the noun is singular, and plural if the meaning
of the noun is plural.   (Compare paragraph 11, above.)

The class has voted to invite a hundred guests to *its* annual
dance.
The class rose from *their* chairs.
The council has changed the date of *its* meeting.
The council were shaking hands with *their* constituents.

Exercise 51.   Agreement of Verb and Pronoun

Choose the proper form in parentheses and explain your
choice.

1. That stack of magazines (belong, belongs) to John.
2. There (was, were) sixty-three people at the dinner.
3. The large picture by Corot, together with the frame, (sell,
sells) for twenty-five dollars.
4. Frank and his dog (was, were) running up the hill.
5. Each of us (has, have) given a dollar for the fund.
6. The little group of old men around the stove (was, were)
smoking corncob pipes.
7. A man's richest possession in his old age (is, are) his memories.
8. Sarah as well as Ruth and Anna (has, have) been invited
to the dance.
9. Either Joe or his brother (is, are) going to college next fall.
10. In one corner of the park (was, were) several beds of old-
fashioned flowers.
11. Every child in the room stood beside (his, her, their) (desk,
desks).

12. John gave a ticket to each of the boys who (is, are) going to the show.

13. We met that man yesterday, but now he (don't, doesn't) know us.

14. A bouquet of large red and white roses (was, were) in a tall vase on the living-room table.

15. Ice cream with thick, dark chocolate syrup (was, were) served after the meeting.

16. Neither of the boys (was, were) able to swim ten yards.

17. Neither the front wheels nor the axle (was, were) damaged.

18. Every member of the band will have (his, their) uniform by next Tuesday.

19. One of the best essays that (was, were) submitted in the contest was written by a freshman.

20. Everybody rose from (his, her, their) (chair, chairs) and applauded.

21. It is useless for him, who (don't, doesn't) know ten words of French, to attend a French university.

22. Either the two Carter boys or their father (is, are) going to plant our garden.

23. Neither of those boys took off (his, their) muddy rubbers.

24. Every horse, cow, and pig on the farm (was, were) gradually dying from lack of food and water.

25. Men, women, and children, dressed in gay colors, (was, were) going to the carnival.

Exercise 52. Agreement of Verb and Pronoun

Correct any errors of agreement in the following exercise and explain the reason for your correction.

One Fourth of July when Don and I were ranching in Montana, Pete suggested that we relieve the tedium by hunting rattlesnakes on the slope of the mesa a couple of miles away. Since we had a holiday, most of the men had gone to town for the big celebration, leaving only six of us with nothing to do except a few chores. In this group was two who had been born and reared in the West and had worked many years on ranches in the region. Pete Champion, the older of the two, had been a sheepherder; but he was now a sub-foreman on this large ranch, where one of the chief occupations were that of raising hay to be fed to sheep in the long, cold winters. The other, Frank Trendon, a wiry, active man of about thirty-five years, had been a cowboy in another part of the state; but now he was in charge of the large herd of horses, many of which was unbroken broncos. Being an excellent rider, he often took part in bronco-busting contests at fairs and rodeos. He still has the reputation of being one of the best riders who has been seen at the state fair. Each of these men, because of their long experience in ranching, were known as an "old-timer," though neither were old in years or appearance. The rest of us were youngsters from the East, known as "tender-feet." Our appearance as well as our age were certain to mark us as inexperienced ranch hands. Every one of us, though from different states beyond the Mississippi, were from the city, having met only by chance on this large ranch, where each of the four were seeking adventure. Though Don and I were chums who had come out together, he lived in Chicago, and I lived in Cincinnati. Ted Ledeman was from Boston, and Sam Chariton from Philadelphia. Before they came west on this trip, neither were ever out of their own state. Since their home cities were the farthest east, all of us first called them "the eastern brothers," and later merely "the brothers."

When Pete proposed the expedition against the rattlesnakes, Frank was eager to go; but the rest of us, being tenderfeet, were hesitant. As we discovered afterwards, every one of us, without exchanging a thought, were suspecting that the old-timers were trying to haze us. After each of them, however, assured us that they were serious, we agreed to go. Since we did not have hightop leather boots to protect our legs, I was uneasy; but neither the brothers, who were usually timid, nor Don were the least afraid. As a precaution, however, I put on a pair of leather puttees that I had found in the bunk house; and each of the other three wrapped burlap around their legs. Then we got a strong club apiece and hiked to the mesa. The club, together with our improvised leggings, were our chief protection.

On the slope of this mesa there was layers of flat rock protruding like steps, under which was large cracks and pockets where the snakes had their nests. On the bright days they came out upon the flat rocks, as upon front porches, to take their sun baths. Being somewhat indolent when engaged in this pastime, they were supposed to be less dangerous than usual. Soon we discovered, however, that they were amply protected, because the color of the rock, as well as that of the occasional clumps of grass and sagebrush, were so much like their own that they were nearly invisible. Not knowing when one might unexpectedly attack us or when we might even step on one, we proceeded warily. I could see that the brothers were as uneasy as I was; but neither the old-timers nor Don were showing any signs of nervousness. I suspected, however, that Don was not so calm as he seemed, because I knew that he was one of those fellows who doesn't readily show his feelings. Every one of the boys were moving forward slowly, first looking all about them and then taking a cautious step. Each had their club raised, prepared to strike quickly. I assumed that I was moving with them, but soon I realized that I had been standing still. When I tried to move, I could not. I had one of those peculiar feelings that comes over nearly everyone when they are bewildered in a strange, dark room and fear that they are about to knock over an expensive vase or perhaps to step into an open pit. The thought of being surrounded by numerous unseen snakes were paralyzing me. In this condition a person is in such a daze, I discovered, that he don't know what is happening. For a second or two I scarcely knew where the other boys were. Then I heard Don call to me, and I suddenly realized that either Frank or Pete were beside me, pointing to the ground. At once I came to life. In front of me, scarcely a yard away, one of those big speckled and striped snakes were crawling out of a hole. I was still frightened, but active. Instinctively defending myself, I began to beat him. Everyone else was beside me, with their club in the air, ready to help; but I needed no one.   When the snake was quite dead and harmless, I discovered that he had eleven rattles, which I cut off as a souvenir.

Later, after I had got over my initial fright, we saw many more big snakes.   Frank and Pete killed several, and each of the other tenderfeet were able to kill at least one.   The old-timers, of course, were out only for the excitement.   The rest of us were, too; but everyone of us were also eager to have some memento.   The rattles of a big snake, we felt, was a trophy of our exploits that we could show to our friends back home.

Case

1. *Case* is the aspect of a substantive which indicates its relationship to a verb, a preposition, or another substantive in the sentence.

2. There are three cases: *nominative, possessive,* and *objective.*

3. Substantives in each of these cases have the following relationships:

CASE	RELATED TO:
Nominative:	verb as subject
	verb as predicate nominative
	another substantive in nominative case as appositive
Possessive:	substantive that names person, thing, or characteristic possessed
Objective:	verb or verbal as object
	preposition as object
	infinitive as subject
	another substantive in objective case as appositive

These relationships are illustrated in the following sentence, in which each substantive is italicized. Below the sentence are given the case and the relationship of each substantive.

> *John's brother, Charles, who* is the *editor* of a well-known *magazine,* is sending *me* to *Mexico,* where *he* expects *me* to find *material* for *my history* of the *Aztecs,* a *people*

of an early *civilization whom Cortez* discovered in the
sixteenth *century*.

SUBSTANTIVE	CASE	RELATED TO:
John's	possessive	substantive, *brother*
brother	nominative	verb, *is sending*, as subject
Charles	nominative	substantive, *brother*, as appositive
who	nominative	verb, *is*, as subject
editor	nominative	verb, *is*, as predicate noun
magazine	objective	preposition, *of*, as object
me	objective	verb, *is sending*, as object
Mexico	objective	preposition, *to*, as object
he	nominative	verb, *expects*, as subject
*me	objective	infinitive, *to find*, as subject
material	objective	infinitive, *to find*, as object
my	possessive	substantive, *history*
history	objective	preposition, *for*, as object
Aztecs	objective	preposition, *of*, as object
people	objective	substantive, *Aztecs*, as appositive
civilization	objective	preposition, *of*, as object
whom	objective	verb, *discovered*, as object
Cortez	nominative	verb, *discovered*, as subject
century	objective	preposition, *in*, as object

* The infinitive phrase, *me to find material*, is the object of *expects*.
Thus it is also a substantive.

The Means of Indicating Case

4. In some languages a substantive has a different form
to indicate each of the cases. In modern English, however, it does not. The noun, the personal pronoun, and
who as relative and interrogative pronoun have different
forms; but of these only the personal pronoun has many,
though even it does not have one for each case. The
changes in these three classes of substantives are shown
in the following tables:

NOUNS

	SINGULAR	PLURAL	SINGULAR	PLURAL
Nominative	girl	girls	man	men
Possessive	girl's	girls'	man's	men's
Objective	girl	girls	man	men

WHO

	SINGULAR AND PLURAL
Nominative	who
Possessive	whose
Objective	whom

PERSONAL PRONOUNS

First Person

	SINGULAR	PLURAL
Nominative	I	we
Possessive	my or mine	our or ours
Objective	me	us

Second Person

	SINGULAR	PLURAL
Nominative	you	you
Possessive	your or yours	your or yours
Objective	you	you

Third Person

	SINGULAR Masculine	Feminine	Neuter	PLURAL All Genders
Nominative	he	she	it	they
Possessive	his	her or hers	its	their or theirs
Objective	him	her	it	them

5. The change in the form of any word in order to express its person, gender, number, or case is called an *inflection* of the word. A systematic table showing the

complete inflection of a substantive, like any one of the foregoing, is called a *declension*. To state the declension of a substantive is *to decline* the substantive.

6. Ordinarily you will have no trouble with case, but in a few perplexing uses you may need special guidance.

Case of Pronouns

7. The case of a pronoun is not affected by the case of its antecedent, although the two may happen to be in the same case. It must always be in the case needed to express its own relationship to a verb, a preposition, or another noun in its own clause. Note the usage in the following sentences:

> John returned this morning. He has been in New York. (*He* is in the same case as the antecedent, *John*, because each is the subject of the clause in which it occurs.)

> John returned this morning from his vacation in New York. (Since the antecedent, *John*, is the subject of its clause, it is in the nominative case; but the pronoun, *his*, is in the possessive case, modifying *vacation*.)

> Fred was standing on the chair when it collapsed. (The antecedent, *chair*, which is the object of *on*, is in the objective case; but *it*, the subject of the dependent clause, is in the nominative case.)

> James knows the man who was here yesterday. (The antecedent, *man*, which is the object of *knows*, is in the objective case; but *who*, which is the subject of its clause, is in the nominative case.)

> James knows the man whom Bob met yesterday. (*Man* is in the objective case because it is the object of *knows;* but its pronoun, *whom*, is in the objective case because it is the object of *met*.)

PERSONAL PRONOUNS

8. In most usages the case of a personal pronoun is obvious, but a few constructions cause some difficulties that are explained in this section.

9. When a personal pronoun is used as a predicate nominative, it must be in the nominative case:

> It is *I*.
> The new member is *he*.
> The author of this poem is *she*.
> The officers of the club are John and *I*.
> The officers are *he* and *I*.
> The two important characters in the play are *they*.

The case of the pronouns in all of the foregoing sentences is correct. There is a decided tendency for people to use *me* in the first sentence, *It is me*, and some writers maintain that this usage is common enough to be called correct; but most careful writers do not use it, and few grammarians accept it. The use of the nominative case of pronouns in constructions represented by the other sentences is unquestioned. If, however, the case seems awkward, the structure of the sentence may be changed, probably as in the following sentences, though this change shifts the emphasis:

> She is the author of this poem.
> He and I are the officers.
> They are the two important characters in the play.

10. The object of a verb or a preposition must of course be in the objective case. Errors frequently occur when the object is compound, with one or more pronouns among its members. Observe the following examples of correct usage:

> I saw your *brother* and *him* at the game.
> Father took *Charles* and *me* to the concert.
> We took *her* and *him* with us.
> My brother gave *him* and *me* tickets to the game.
> Jim sent my *sister* and *me* a box of candy.
> Jim sent *her* and *me* a box of candy.
> These tickets are for *you* and *us*.
> I shall divide this cake equally between *her* and *him*.
> What the program will be is a secret between *them* and *us*.

If you are not alert in writing these compound objects, you may put the second object in the nominative case, especially when the case of the first member is not expressed by a definite form, as in *Father took Charles and me* or *These tickets are for you and us.*

11. The subject of an infinitive (see Study Unit 15, paragraph 20) must be in the objective case.

> We expected *her* to sing in the choir.
> Mother asked *me* to help her.
> My instructor told *me* to write the sentence on the board.
> Jim saw *him* break the glass.   (The infinitive is *break*, with *to* omitted.)
> We heard *him* drop his books.   (The infinitive is *drop*, with *to* omitted.)

In these sentences the object of the predicate verb is not the pronoun following it, but the whole infinitive phrase — sometimes called an infinitive clause — of which the pronoun is the subject. The thought of the first sentence, for example, is not "We expected *her*," but "We expected *her to sing in the choir.*"

12. When a personal pronoun is used as a predicate nominative following the infinitive *to be*, it must be in the objective case if the infinitive has a subject. It must be in the nominative case, however, if the infinitive does not have a subject. The reason is that a predicate nominative must agree with the subject. Since the subject of an infinitive must be in the objective case, the subject of *to be* must be in this case. The predicate pronoun, therefore, must also be in the objective case, as in the following example:

> They took *him* to be *me.*

In the following sentence, however, *to be* does not have a subject, and so the predicate pronoun is in the nominative case, as it usually is after any form of this verb, such as *is, am,* or *was:*

> The author appears to be *he.*

The infinitive *to be* is used as a predicate adjective to modify *author;* and *he*, the predicate pronoun related to the infinitive *to be*, completes the modification.

13. A personal pronoun agrees in case with a noun with which it is in apposition.

> That boy, *he* in the tan sweater, is president of our class. (*He* is in the nominative case, agreeing with *boy*, the subject of the sentence.)
>
> Do you see that boy, him in the tan sweater? (*Him* is in the objective case, agreeing with *boy*, the object of the sentence.)

14. Mistakes frequently occur in sentences in which a personal pronoun has an appositive. Study carefully the following sentences:

> The teacher questioned *us boys* for ten minutes. (Note well that the case of the pronoun is not changed by the fact that it has a noun appositive. With the appositive or without it, the pronoun is the object of the verb and must be in the objective case.)
>
> Several of *us fellows* went to the game. (The pronoun is in the objective case because it is the object of a preposition; *fellows* is in apposition with it.)
>
> Let's *you and me* go home. (This sentence without the contraction and with the subject expressed is, of course, *You let us, you and me, go home.* Since *us* is in the objective case, its appositives *you* and *me* must be also. Note, however, that *us* is in the objective case not because it is the object of *let*, but because it is the subject of the infinitive *go*.)

15. When a personal pronoun is used in an elliptical clause introduced by *than* or *as*, its case is the same as it would be if the clause were complete. Note, for example, the following sentence:

> John is younger than **I.**

The elliptical clause, including the conjunction, is merely *than I*. Completed, the clause is *than I am* or *than I am young*. Similarly, the case of the pronouns in the following elliptical clauses must be determined:

> Ruth earns higher grades than I (earn).
> Frank is as tall as he (is).

Consider the different meanings of the following pairs of sentences:

> George gave Fred more than me. (With the objective case the sentence means *George gave Fred more than he gave me.*)
> George gave Fred more than I. (With the nominative case the sentence means *George gave Fred more than I gave him.*)
> You ought to be able to accompany him as well as me. (This sentence means *You ought to be able to accompany him as well as you are able to accompany me.*)
> You ought to be able to accompany him as well as I. (This sentence means *You ought to be able to accompany him as well as I am able to accompany him.*)

PERPLEXING USES OF WHO

16. Since *who* alone of a group of similar pronouns — *that*, *which*, and *what* — has a different form for each case, it is the only one likely to cause any difficulty in the use of case. (What is said here about *who* applies also to *whoever* and *whosoever*.)

17. The case of *who*, whether used as a relative or as an interrogative pronoun, is always determined by its relationship to other words in its own clause. Usually this relationship is easy to determine.

> The man *who* called yesterday is here again. (*Who* is the subject of *called*.)
> The man *whom* you met yesterday is my father. (*Whom* is the object of *met*.)
> *Whom* did you speak to? (*Whom* is the object of *to*.)

18. There are, however, two constructions that may mislead you when you are writing sentences:

a. When a *who* clause is the object of a verb or a preposition, you must be careful not to mistake the pronoun for the object of the verb or preposition.

> I know who is coming to visit us. (The whole clause is the object of *know; who* is the subject of *is coming*.)
>
> I know who he is. (The clause is the object of *know; who* is the predicate pronoun in the clause, and hence is in the nominative case.)
>
> I know whom you have invited. (Again, the clause is the object of *know; whom* is in the objective case because it is the object of *have invited*.)
>
> We lent the book to whoever wanted it. (The object of *to* is the whole dependent clause, of which the subject is *whoever*.)
>
> He sent a copy of his book to whomever he knew. (Again, the object of *to* is the entire dependent clause; *whomever* is in the objective case, not as the object of *to*, but as the object of *knew*.)

b. When *who* is followed by a short parenthetical clause that is not set off by commas, such as *we thought, he thinks, did you say*, you must be careful not to mistake *who* for the object of the verb of the inserted clause.

> Who did you say came today? (*Who* is the subject of *came*. The inserted clause *did you say* is parenthetical.)
>
> He is the man *who* we thought was chairman. (*Who* is the subject of *was*, not the object of *thought*. *We thought* is an inserted clause, as you can see if you set it off by commas.)
>
> He is the man whom we thought you had elected chairman. (*Whom* is in the objective case, not because it is the object of *thought*, but because it is the object of *had elected*.)

He is the man whom we thought to be chairman. (Here *we thought* is not parenthetical. *Thought* is the predicate verb of the relative clause, with an infinitive phrase as object. *Whom* is in the objective case, not because it is the object of *thought*, but because it is the subject of the infinitive *to be*.)

Possessive Case of Nouns

19. A noun expresses possession by means of the possessive or by means of the preposition *of*, as follows:

> There is the man's house.
> There is the house of the man.

20. The preposition *of* is generally used with nouns naming inanimate objects:

> The surface of the street was worn. (Not: *The street's surface was worn.*)
> The door of the cabin was broken. (Not: *The cabin's door was broken.*)

21. Exceptions to the foregoing principle, however, are nouns expressing *space* or *time* or *personification*. These generally use the possessive case:

> We have a full day's task ahead of us.
> Our house is an hour's ride from town.
> John has received his first week's wages.
> Writing the book required a year's work.
> We listened to the ocean's roar.
> The violent storm revealed nature's ruthlessness.

22. Sometimes *of* is used with the possessive of both nouns and pronouns, as in the following sentences:

> A friend of John's sent us this book.
> Here is a new book of mine.
> Being a friend of his, you should vote for Bob.

> I sat up until midnight reading a book of Fred's.
>
> *The Old Wives' Tale* is an important novel of Arnold Bennett's.

Possessive with a Gerund

23. A noun or pronoun preceding and modifying a gerund should be in the possessive case:

> John had not seen the notice of his passing the examination.
>
> Mother objects to my going to Brazil next summer.
>
> Frank was annoyed by Mr. Gordon's laughing at my speech.

In these sentences, you notice, the object of the verb or preposition is the gerund, not the preceding noun or pronoun. In the last, for instance, Frank was not annoyed by Mr. Gordon, but by the laughing done by Mr. Gordon.

24. You must not confuse this type of sentence, however, with a similar one in which the verbal is a participle. Note the difference in the following pairs of sentences:

> I don't like his asking you to go to the dance. (Here *asking* is a gerund, the object of the verb *like*. *His* modifies *asking*.)
>
> I heard him asking you to go to the dance. (In this sentence *him* is the object of *heard*, and *asking* is a participle modifying *him*. The purpose is not to emphasize that I heard *asking*, but that I heard *him;* and when I heard him, he was asking.)
>
> Father was pleased about Mary's playing in the orchestra. (*Playing* is a gerund, object of *about*. *Mary's* modifies *playing*.)
>
> Father heard Mary playing in the orchestra. (*Mary* is the object of *heard;* and *playing* is a participle modifying *Mary*.)

Exercise 53.   Case

Give the case of each italicized word in the following
sentences and state the reason for your answer.

1. On this trip we visited the people *who* were here last
   summer.
2. We know *whom* you visited last summer.
3. *Who* did you say gave you that pen?
4. The coach asked *him* to be captain.
5. Jane is a better violinist than her sisters because she
   practices more than *they.*
6. My roommate last year was *he.*
7. Isabelle asked *us* to go to the picnic.
8. Let's you and *me* study for the quiz.
9. The best actor seems to be *he.*
10. *Whom* did you give the book to?
11. Laura invited *us* boys to her party.
12. Jack asked *us* boys to go fishing with him.
13. This is an agreement now between you and *me.*
14. I was in doubt about *whom* I should invite to the dance.
15. I was in doubt about *whom* I lent the book to.
16. Do you know the man about *whom* we were talking?
17. I met the man *whom* you are talking about.
18. We are in doubt about *who* he is.
19. John is as able to do this work as *I.*
20. Father asked us, John and *me,* to spade the garden.
21. I heard of *John's* climbing the mountain yesterday.
22. We have done a long *day's* work.
23. *Whom* do you intend to visit in Baltimore?
24. Several of *us* fellows drove to Chicago last summer.
25. We were shown the exhibit by a man *whom* we took to be
    an official guide.

EXERCISE 54. Case

Correct all errors of case in the following exercise and state the reasons for your corrections.

My first experience in being the victim of a practical joke was when I was a freshman at an inexpensive boys' boarding school, where all of we boys, most of who were from farms and small towns, earned our board and room by helping to maintain the buildings and grounds. We did all of the janitor work and gardening, and we assisted with the cooking and baking. The special jobs were given for the year to whomever was qualified; but the others were assigned periodically, generally every day, to different boys. We freshmen, nearly all of who had just left grade school, were conspicuously helpless in doing any kind of work; but the seniors, who the faculty and upperclassmen had trained for three years, were usually more competent than us; and so they were the supervisors. Some of we younger fellows, whenever we were given unpleasant tasks, naturally envied the seniors their preferred positions. We were sure that we could supervise the work as well as them; but since a tradition demanded that seniors who were in charge of work must be obeyed, we grumbled a little among ourselves, but did what they told us. We knew that if the director of the school had heard of us grumbling, he would have reprimanded us; and since he had eyes that withered us even in our casual interviews, we preferred to maintain friendly relations between him and we.

The method of assigning the odd jobs to us underclassmen was quite simple. Every day following our lunch, while all of we fellows were in the dining hall, the head senior, whom the director had appointed to serve for one week, read the names of those whom were to work that day. Then each reported to the senior whom was in charge of his task and did as much as he could until he had to get ready for his first afternoon class at two o'clock. If anyone was fortunate enough to escape an assignment, he was free to do as he pleased. For this reason, when the head senior rose, every-one was silent and tense, listening nervously to the reading of the names and hoping that his would not be mentioned. The senior, too, was as nervous as us, but for a different reason. He knew that his task was not popular; and, furthermore, he had had no experience in speaking before a large group, es-pecially a group of his contemporaries whom he felt were hostile to him. For these reasons, some of the seniors spoke so indistinctly that we did not know who of us he had assigned to a job. As a result, we sometimes got into trouble for failing unwittingly to do our work.

In the second week of my first year, for example, when all of we freshmen were inexperienced and the senior was even more nervous than us, this situation considerably embarrassed my roommate and I. After the names had been read and all of us were leaving the dining hall, Jim and me congratulated ourselves for having escaped, and then trotted off to the athletic field for a game of baseball. We did not clearly under-stand what the senior had said, but we were certain that he had not mentioned our names. Within half an hour, however, another freshman came running down the field, calling for Tom Kelsall. After I had said that I was him, he told me that the director wanted Jim and I to come to his office at once. Seeing that he was excited and apparently serious, I asked him what was wrong. Between gasps for breath he answered that he did not know, but thought there was some trouble about us not reporting for work. An upperclassman, he said, had ordered him to tell us, but he didn't know whom the upperclassman was.

When we entered the director's private office, we were trembling too much to speak. Fortunately, he was standing by the window, with his back toward us; and so we had time in which to calm ourselves. As the door clicked shut, he turned slowly and stared at we two flushed and frightened youngsters. He was the kind of man whom the older boys said pretended to be more austere than he was, but we were believing him to be entirely serious. We wished only that we could seem to be as calm as him.

After a couple of seconds, he asked, "What may I do for you?"

We were more concerned about what he was going to do to us, but Jim stuttered, "We were told that you wanted Tom and I to come here."

"Who told you," he asked, still austerely, "that I wanted you?"

"A boy," I answered, "who sits at the table next to ours in the dining hall. I don't know who he is. He said that some-one, an upperclassman, had sent him to tell us."

"Did he say whom the upperclassman was?"

"No, he didn't," Jim answered; "and neither of we had time to ask anyone else."

Why he was torturing us, I could not understand. He was like a cat with his mice, teasing the two of us, whom he knew could not get away.

"So," he went on, "you don't know whom either of them was. Do you know, by any chance, what I want with you?"

"No, sir," I answered, now really trembling. "I don't know for sure, sir; but this boy said it was about us going to play when the head senior had told Jim and I to report for work."

"I see," he said, looking less austere, I thought, though I expected him to be furious. "Why didn't you do what Larchmont told you to do?" Larchmont was the senior.

"But, sir," I spoke up, "he didn't tell us. We were sure. He didn't speak distinctly, but we listened carefully, and we didn't hear him call our names."

Just then I was conscious of numerous voices outside, and I thought that the director was smiling; but I couldn't be sure.

"You are positive that you didn't hear him call your names?"

"Positive," we both said. "Positive."

"Well, then," he said, pleasantly, even rather sympatheti-cally, "you may go."

When we got outside, we found out what the voices were. About fifty of the boys, grouped in front of the entrance to the building, burst out laughing; and then Jim and I knew that they had played a joke on us.

Exercise 55. Review Exercise

Group the following words properly by giving the appropriate mark of punctuation to be used at the end of each complete sentence and between coordinate clauses. Then correct all faults in grammar that occur within the sentences and explain your corrections.

Have you ever drove over a wet clay road before any ruts were made if you have not you have missed an adventure but it is an adventure that you can afford to miss I know what I am talking about because I have had the experience and I shall not forget it it happened on June 7 if anyone had warned me of the risks I probably would not have took the chance but I am not sure I suspect that most people seldom heed warnings therefore I am not warning you I merely want to assure you that I never shall repeat the experience I do not object of course to driving through ordinary mud but this mud you must know was different it was both slippery and sticky reminding me somewhat of melted chewing gum I have said that the road was made of clay however I doubt that "clay" is the proper word it probably was made of gumbo which is a kind of soil that is like powder when it is dry and like axle grease and gum when it is wet.

Fortunately I was not alone on this trip my roommate and two of our friends were with me all of us were going to New York for the summer where we had jobs waiting for us since we were afraid that they would not be held for us we did not want to lose any time otherwise we should not have got into the mud every one of us now realize that we should have waited until the roads dried in fact my roommate John was his name suggested that we wait at least until the rain stopped but neither the other two fellows nor I were willing to listen to him I might have taken his advice if the weather report in the local newspaper which I had read the night before had not predicted clear weather furthermore the roads over which we had traveled for the two preceding days looked so good that not any of we three was able to imagine how a few hours of rain could of made them muddy to back up my opinion I made some inquiries and of all the people who I asked only one advised us not to go this one man looked at me a bit roguishly then he calmly remarked that the road was open to whomever cared to go over it in spite of this obvious warning we went.

I agreed to drive because John said that something he had ate for breakfast made him feel badly, and our companions complained that they were worn out from the preceding day's drive John I knew was one of those fellows who is always nursing himself and so I did not urge him to drive what I suspected however was that both of our companions and John was afraid to drive since I could not deny that I felt well I took the wheel soon we were at the end of the paved city street the road ahead of us which was the main east and west highway seemed to stretch for miles it was as smooth as glass and it looked good nevertheless I suspected that it was treacherous consequently I gripped the wheel firmly braced myself carefully and drove boldly forward suddenly I had the odd sensation of holding tightly to a steering wheel that was not connected to anything for regardless of how I turned the wheel the car took its own zigzag path down the road it was one of those helpless feelings that is experienced occasionally in terrible dreams when one tries to call for help and cannot utter a sound the car turned across the road and headed for a five-foot ditch that was along the side I turned the wheels but the car kept sliding we were within a foot of the edge so that only a slight skid would put us over everyone held their breath but not any of us were afraid that is not anyone said that they were afraid fortunately the car stopped upon the crumpling edge of the bank then I backed it got it out of the ruts and drove it forward again after that experience all of we fellows were sorry that we came we should of turned around and went back if we had not been afraid of getting into the ditch therefore we crept forward at five miles an hour wondering how far we were from the next town for miles in front of us we could see nothing but mud one of our companions said that there was mud to the front of us mud to the rear of us and mud to the side of us then John recited those familiar lines from Tennyson's "Charge of the Light Brigade" you recall them do you not I said that I was reminded more of a few lines from Coleridge's "Ancient Mariner" do you know the ones that I refer to they are as follows "Water water everywhere nor any drop to drink" well these kind of remarks revived our good spirits but I could not keep from thinking about how much time we were losing we had hoped to be in Kansas City by dark and it already was nearly noon an hour later however the rain stopped the sun came out and the roads soon dried all of us then were relieved of a three-hour nervous tension we had had no physical mishap though we had been upon the brink of one but we had had a grueling mental experience all of us have marked June 7 as a red-letter day in our lives and everyone is certain that what they remember most distinctly is the vastness of the mud and their feeling of complete helplessness.

EXERCISE 56. Review Exercise

Group the following words properly by giving the appropriate mark of punctuation to be used at the end of each complete sentence and between coordinate clauses. Then correct all faults in grammar that occur within the sentences and explain your corrections.

One summer between my sophomore and junior years in college I was in a type of accident that I am not likely to experience again I was with a classmate Walter Payson who all of we boys called "Lunar" because of his round smiling face which resembled a full moon the two of us were traveling through the western Appalachian mountains selling books in order to earn enough money for he and I to go to college again the next year though nearly as rugged as those in the eastern range these mountains are not so high as them in fact they are only hills but they were mountains to both of we fellows who had been reared in the flat country where a little knoll as big as a haystack was called a hill what made them impressive was not their size so much as their number the whole region was one hill after another each covered with big green trees and dense underbrush it was one of those sections of the country that was then spoken of as "backward" because it was sparsely settled and only slightly cultivated living far apart on the sides of hills or in narrow valleys the people seemed satisfied with mere existence they cleared a little ground for a cabin and small garden apparently they raised only enough food for their own use to get a little money with which to buy what they could not grow or make many of them planted small patches of tobacco which seemed to be the principal crop of the region here and there among the hills were little dilapidated villages inhabited by indifferent people whose range of interests were as limited as the farmer's there was a few untidy stores with offices above them occupied according to the signs on the dirty windows by lawyers doctors and dentists but neither they nor the storekeepers was ever busy everyone looked as though they had nothing important to do from morning until night in the heat of the day every one of them were laying on the grass or setting on benches under the big trees in the cool evenings many of them were playing games for example when we drove into a town late one afternoon we found both men and boys out in the street playing marbles we could scarce believe our eyes professional men and merchants crawling around in the middle of the main street we had never saw before regions of these kind obviously were not profitable markets for our books before we left home my father who had been in this part of the country warned us that we could not make our expenses and Lunar's father was definitely opposed to us going but neither of we two were convinced we naturally thought that each of them were old-fashioned furthermore we felt obliged to go the publishing company having assigned us the territory we wanted to do our best with it. "Let's you and I show them," said Lunar, "that we can do well."

Our plan was to divide the work between Lunar and I neither of us were well qualified for the job but I had had more experience in selling than him therefore we agreed that I should sell and he would keep the accounts and mail the orders the two of we however always went together to call on a prospective customer I always felt more confident when he was along moreover he was now and then able to help me make a sale though generally even my best effort together with his arguments were not enough most of the people who we called on did not want to buy one of our books or did not have any money to spare some of them even the more prosperous villagers who we tried to sell thought that books of any kind was a luxury nevertheless we proceeded diligently to cover the territory first we called on all of the prospects in the largest village a settlement of about five hundred people then we hired a horse and buggy automobiles not being in common use at that time and drove into the country trying to sell a book to whomever seemed to be willing to listen to us every morning we went out on our day's drive returning sometimes too late for supper.

On one of these daily trips we had our accident it happened in the late morning probably at noon as we were approaching the top of a hill on a narrow dusty road which had been cut into the side of the hill the day being hot neither we nor the horse were energetic in fact each of us, Lunar and me, were setting in a corner of the seat half asleep probably I should say that we were laying on the seat because we had stretched out as far as we could supporting ourselves with our feet against the dashboard the horse was plodding on listlessly sending up a little cloud of dust as we were rounding a curve I noticed him raise his head sharply and so I raised up to see what was wrong with him then I heard a rumbling and a shout I assumed that a wagon was approaching us but the hill obstructing my view of the road I could not be sure about what was coming how two vehicles could pass on this narrow road was beyond my understanding nevertheless I drove as close as

I could to the side of the hill and stopped then I nudged Lunar whom I noticed had gone to sleep as he raised up to inquire with feigned annoyance whom I thought I was punching a team of oxen came trudging around the curve pulling a wagon loaded with lumber setting on top of it was the driver a man who I took to be about sixty years of age when he saw our horse and buggy he became as excited as us he pulled on his reins and shouted to the oxen to stop but each of them merely lowered their heads and snorted then they lunged forward madly the driver trying frantically to keep his wagon on the road and to keep it from hitting our buggy that he almost succeeded was a miracle as the wagon passed us it swerved slightly so that it bumped our rear wheel the impact nearly knocking Lunar and I out of the buggy gaining our equilibrium we merely set upright staring at each other neither of us were able to move or speak we must of looked like statues then Lunar being one of those good-natured fellows who is always amused began to laugh the spell being broken I laughed also without exchanging a word both of us jumped out of the buggy to see how much it had been damaged being somewhat pessimistic I naturally thought that it had been ruined furthermore I was wondering who we could get in this lonely region to repair it neither of we two I knew were able to drive a nail straight our careful inspection however soon disclosed that the only damage were two broken spokes this was not serious enough we decided to prevent us using the buggy moreover the horse was in good condition in our excitement we had forgotten about him but we were grateful that he had behaved splendidly snorting oxen were so common on the roads I suppose that he was accustomed to them since neither the horse nor us was injured we agreed to resume our trip however after we had gone a few miles the damaged wheel was wobbling so much that we decided to return to the village neither of we wanted to be stranded all night in the hills nor did we care for any unpleasantness with the owner of the livery stable who we knew from experience had a bad disposition both of us said that if he would let Lunar and I pay for the damage and then say nothing more about it we should be satisfied the old man with the lumber wagon of course should of paid but where he went we did not know nor did we ever find out as I now recall how madly those two oxen were charging down the road I suspect that they are still running probably racing through eternity on a cloud of dust.

INDEX